Newman

Past Masters

AQUINAS Anthony Kenny
ARISTOTLE Jonathan Barnes
FRANCIS BACON Anthony Quinton
BAYLE Elisabeth Labrousse
BERKELEY J. O. Urmson
BURKE C. B. Macpherson
CARLYLE A. L. Le Quesne
CLAUSEWITZ Michael Howard
COBBETT Raymond Williams
COLERIDGE Richard Holmes
CONFUCIUS Raymond Dawson
DANTE George Holmes
DARWIN Jonathan Howard
ENGELS Terrell Carver

GALILEO Stillman Drake
HEGEL Peter Singer
HOMER Jasper Griffin
HUME A. J. Ayer
JESUS Humphrey Carpenter
KANT Roger Scruton
MACHIAVELLI Quentin Skinner
MARX Peter Singer
MONTAIGNE Peter Burke
NEWMAN Owen Chadwick
PASCAL Alban Krailsheimer
PLATO R. M. Hare
PROUST Derwent May
TOLSTOY Henry Gifford

Forthcoming

AUGUSTINE Henry Chadwick
BACH Denis Arnold
BERGSON Leszek Kolakowski
THE BUDDHA Michael Carrithers
JOSEPH BUTLER R. G. Frey
CERVANTES P. E. Russell
CHAUCER George Kane
COPERNICUS Owen Gingerich
DIDEROT Peter France
GEORGE ELIOT Rosemary Ashton
ERASMUS James McConica
GIBBON J. W. Burrow
GODWIN Alan Ryan
GOETHE T. J. Reed
HERZEN Aileen Kelly
JEFFERSON Jack P. Greene
JOHNSON Pat Rogers

LAMARCK L. J. Jordanova
LEIBNIZ G. M. Ross
LINNAEUS W. T. Stearn
LOCKE John Dunn
MENDEL Vitezslav Orel
MILL William Thomas
THOMAS MORE Anthony Kenny
WILLIAM MORRIS Peter Stansky
MUHAMMAD Michael Cook
NEWTON P. M. Rattansi
PETRARCH Nicholas Mann
RUSKIN George P. Landow
SHAKESPEARE Germaine Greer
ADAM SMITH D. D. Raphael
SOCRATES Bernard Williams
VICO Peter Burke

and others

Owen Chadwick

NEWMAN

Oxford   New York

OXFORD UNIVERSITY PRESS

1983

Oxford University Press, Walton Street, Oxford OX2 6DP

London Glasgow New York Toronto
Delhi Bombay Calcutta Madras Karachi
Kuala Lumpur Singapore Hong Kong Tokyo
Nairobi Dar es Salaam Cape Town
Melbourne Auckland

and associates in
Beirut Berlin Ibadan Mexico City Nicosia

First published 1983 as an Oxford University Press paperback
and simultaneously in a hardback edition

British Library Cataloguing in Publication Data
Chadwick, Owen
Newman. — (Past masters) 1801-1890
1. Newman, John Henry 2. Theology, Catholic
I. Title II. Series
230'.2'0924 BX4705.N5
ISBN 0-19-287568-X
ISBN 0-19-287567-1 Pbk

Set by Datamove Ltd
Printed in Great Britain by
Cox & Wyman Ltd,
Reading

Contents

Abbreviations

A   *Apologia pro vita sua*
C   *On Consulting the Faithful in Matters of Doctrine*
D   *Discussions and Arguments*
Diff   *Difficulties of Anglicans*
G   *An Essay in Aid of a Grammar of Assent*
I   *The Idea of a University*
L   *Letters and Diaries of J. H. Newman*
M   *Two Essays on Miracles*
O   *On the Inspiration of Scripture*
P   *Parochial and Plain Sermons*
S   *Sermons Preached before the University of Oxford*
V   *The Via Media of the Anglican Church*

References are given by (volume and) page to Newman's own uniform edition of his works, except in the case of A, C, I, L and T, where reference is made to the editions specified in the list of further reading on p. 79.

1 Introduction

John Henry Newman was an eminent Victorian despite himself. He wrote two books still regarded as classics of English prose. He led a religious movement in the Church of England which transformed the worship of that Church and helped to alter the ways of other Protestant Churches. He helped Britain to see for the first time since the Reformation that Catholic priests could be as humane, and generous, and unbigoted, as anyone else. He had the most interesting idea of the nature of faith propounded by any thinker of the nineteenth century. He was the first theorist of Christian doctrine to face the challenge of modern historical enquiry. And he was a quiet unpretentious man of prayer. All that is more than enough justification for his appearance in a series of Past Masters.

Another eminent Victorian, Thomas Carlyle, was very contemptuous of Newman and Newman's intellect. But if the two men entered a competition for delicacy of thought, or for depth, Newman would win comfortably. They were both rhetoricians. But if a prize were offered for the worse rhetorician, Carlyle would win comfortably.

Why these condemnations, which come from others besides Carlyle?

Half-way through his life, on 9 October 1845, at Littlemore near Oxford, Newman was received by a travelling Italian priest and became a Roman Catholic. The world of the nineteenth century was opening its mind amid new discoveries in science or history, new investigation in philosophy. The fresh air of the intellect was very exciting. The Roman Catholic Church of the nineteenth century was occupied in closing its mind. It shrank from this new knowledge. It felt horror at evolution, officially condemned toleration, saw many of its best historians leave its embrace in disgust at its attitude to history, and tried to stop any good Catholic from belonging to the political left. It centralised nearly everything under the papacy in Rome. And the papacy, threatened by a new Italy, was as illiberal and reactionary as possible. Newman, educated a Protestant, a famous Oxford don with a large following of young men in the University, chose to submit his mind to this reaction. Thomas Carlyle said that Newman had not the brains of a moderate-sized rabbit.

And Newman boasted of this submission. The word *liberalism* then stood for freedom of the citizen, for toleration of other people's opinions, for intelligent open-mindedness, for a welcome to the new discoveries of science or history. Newman kept on saying that he dedicated his life to the fight against *liberalism*. He not only joined a reactionary institution but made frequent public profession that he was himself a leading reactionary.

The Churches of the Victorian century had a very good time and simultaneously a bad time. They had a good time in attendance, morale, feeling of advance, conviction that society was growing more Christian. The growing population filled their churches with people and their hearts with excitement. The Roman Catholics were only one instance of a general contentment among the Churches. Irish immigrants, fleeing from famine or in search of work, poured into the country and the little Catholic chapels overflowed. Newman's most eloquent (though far below his best) sermon *The Second Spring* (1852) expressed this euphoria which was felt in all the Churches. 'It is the coming in of a Second Spring; it is a restoration in the moral world, such as that which yearly takes place in the physical . . . The world grows old, but the Church is ever young.'

But the Churches also had a bad time. This was mostly because so many people changed their place of dwelling, and moved from country into town, and went away from their family roots and habits of life. About this vast migration Newman could do nothing, except go and be pastoral amid some of the immigrants in a city suburb. The bad time was also caused by unsettlement of minds. During the century most people ceased to believe the Bible to be all true history. Since

Churches had told everyone for centuries that the Bible was all true history, their reputation could not but fall. During the century many people ceased to believe the possibility that 'miracles' can happen nowadays; and that had more than faint echoes in the question whether miracles could ever have happened.

So the Churches, thriving as never for centuries, were suddenly under threat, or felt to be under threat. The French Revolution had shown how a people could desert the religion of their fathers. Was it possible that this could happen in Britain?

In this difficult world for the Christian intelligence, Newman set himself the life-work of maintaining the force of apostolic Christianity. This meant for him four different sorts of effort:

1 The Christian life must be made real. The only argument for Christianity that proves anything is that it works. If Christians preach self-sacrifice and oppress the poor, their faith is meaningless. Christ will only be real to the world if his disciples follow.

2 Faith must consider its link with philosophy. Can you prove that God exists? Yes, said the eighteenth century; therefore all wise men have faith. But suppose that new discoveries make it harder to *prove* that God exists — suppose Darwin comes along with the idea of evolution or historians point to the contradictions in the gospel texts — do all wise men lose their faith? Evidently not. Then faith cannot be overturned by argument? What is faith?

3 Science must be free. History must be free. No one should be able to suggest that the Church's maltreatment of Galileo, for saying that the Earth went round the Sun, was typical of Churches in the nineteenth century. Science and history must be freed from the leading strings of dogma.

4 And as a special part of this last, the Roman Catholic Church must be deterred from disappearing into an intellectual ghetto. However suspect to Protestants, the Catholic Church had weight in keeping Europe Christian. If it spent its endeavours killing science, and banning history, and saying that

every word of the Bible was literally true, and looking fanatical, its weight would grow lighter and lighter because ultimately it must lose all influence on general society and retain influence only among its devotees.

These were the aims to which Newman dedicated his life. They were all part of the single task of preserving the force of apostolic Christianity in a world which looked to be about to reject religion as behind the times.

2 The nature of Newman's mind

Newman's sense of continuity

Let us take Newman as deep in his heart he felt himself to be — though he could not quite say so after the change of denomination on 9 October 1845, lest he seem to undervalue among Catholics the new start from Littlemore. Let us take him as a mind of unity; growing, articulating, arranging, acquiring new truth from meditating on old truth or even, though more rarely, from new information found in books; but a man with the same mind all his life; the same despite one conversion at the age of fifteen and another conversion at the age of forty-four; a mind with principles formed early, and then expanded, adapted, recast, and yet recognisably the same principles — so that some of his best writing on subjects which he treated in books as a Roman Catholic is found in books which he wrote as a Protestant. This is not to say that the mind stood still; never was a mind so unceasingly in motion. But the motion was always growth, and never revolution. Occasionally he entered some cul-de-sac of the mind and then retreated. But he needed to retreat far less than most men who think a lot. If he got into what looked like a dead end he would pause, and consider, and peer about, and wait, and finally discover that after all he could see a way forward.

This is not a retrospective view of history adopted so that we can see an embryo cardinal in the Protestant boy converted by an evangelical schoolmaster at a boarding-school in Ealing. On the personal level, the accidents of history guided his course. What would have happened to him if the Fellows of Oriel, including Newman, had elected a different head of their college? What would have happened to Newman if the conservative Sir Robert Peel had managed to stay Prime Minister in a minority government for several months longer and had chosen Newman to be the Regius Professor of Divinity at Oxford in the vacancy of 1836 — far the best appointment that could have been made? What would have happened if the heads of Oxford colleges had possessed an elementary sense of justice in March 1841? What would have happened if the cardinals in Rome had had their way and censured Newman for his teaching? These unprofitable *ifs* are put only as a reminder that Newman's career, and therefore the course of intellectual history, could have taken other courses. But if we take the career as it happened, and the mind as it grew, we are conscious that this intelligence never retraced its steps more than a few paces.

The solitary

Newman was a monk by nature as well as by grace. Born in 1801 and sent to a boarding-school at the age of seven, he lived his remaining eighty-two years in male communities: schools, two Oxford colleges, a 'monastery' at Littlemore, a college at Rome, and the Oratory at Birmingham.

He had no low estimate of marriage. The memory of his own home was affectionate. He recognised that if husband and wife live together faithfully they grow in unselfishness. He loved baptism as a sacrament, because he had happiness in seeing men and women bringing the tiniest souls to God. He confessed that a wife and children are blessings (esp. P 3.299, 2.58).

But for him the unmarried state was the way to which he was called. He had this inkling as early as his teens. By the time that he was a young don the conviction was settled. Thenceforth it never wavered. The unmarried man can give more time to his ministry. When at last he was offered a cardinal's hat, which normally meant work in Rome, he made it a condition of acceptance (politely phrased so as not to look like a condition) that he need not move from his little 'monastery'.

> The holy monks, concealed from men,
> In midnight choir, or studious cell,
> In sultry field, or wintry glen,
> The holy monks, I love them well.

This was a poem of 1850.

Newman's earlier years were the age of romanticism. He was touched by the spirit that found the ruins of monasteries poetic and exalting. When he wrote about monks, he wrote about them with an idealised happiness which was not always very historical, but which spoke volumes about his idea of life. The world is manifold, complex, many men pursuing many objects. The cloister is single-minded; a few men pursuing one object; an enclosure where troubled souls come apart and seek a work that is not mingled with the corruptions of society and which, being undistracted, makes possible adoration day by day; where every day is lived for itself, each hour is complete, where the day's acts are not part of some grand plan or calculation; the soul trying to do God's will moment by moment. Newman loved the romance of monks – the wilderness reclaimed, the hermits with their animal friends, the humble servitors, the stream bubbling among the rocks, the kindly confessors. He made his own later life within a smoky suburb of the least romantic among English cities. And yet, even when he was writing of the poetry of monks, he half-consciously portrayed his idea of his moral vocation; a man for whom heaven is next door, and who does not make plans, nor desires to see more than one step ahead; for whom the day just before him suffices for his duty; and so he does his chores, and prays, and meditates, and studies, and writes, and teaches, and looks again at the Scriptures, where the truths about God come in a divine disorder, like the trees and flowers in the Garden of Eden.

In all his communities he had one close friend: Hurrell Froude at Oxford, Ambrose St John in Littlemore and Rome and Birmingham, young William Neville after Ambrose St John died. A particular friendship was indispensable to Newman's life. But despite this dependence upon one other person, and despite his membership of a community, some quality in his mind is more akin to that of the solitary than that of the monk-in-community; a feeling continuous with his sight as a child of only two beings in the world, himself and his Maker.

Newman was not an outgoing man. He was a man for intimates and friends. As superior of a community he commanded the allegiance of those members of the community who felt that to him they owed their soul. Where they did not feel that, and where they had no natural rapport with him, they found the gulf hard to cross. Sometimes he was very silent; a little because he was shy, but more because he could think of nothing to say. We find members of his community who said that he was cold, or uncommunicative, or lacking in affection, or keeping men at arm's length. We who know more of Newman's interior, and see the affection of the man, are surprised at these verdicts. But they recur too often to be only the carping of small minds. He found the Senior Common Room at Oriel a place of the dullest conversation, and he found the time of recreation among his Oratorians stiff and tedious, and he could think of nothing which would promote intelligent exchange.

When he went into strange company he felt himself to be bashful. One of his friends invented a *mot* that when his mouth was open it seemed as if it would never shut, and when it was shut it seemed as if it would never open. Once when he was staying in Rome, he described how he lived the life of a recluse, and said 'What good would it do to go out?' – and he was thinking not only of his inability to speak fluent Italian but of his feeling that he was tongue-tied. These silences specially afflicted him when he disagreed with the person to whom he talked. When he had a misunderstanding, and then a meeting to clear it up, that meeting sometimes needed another meeting to clear up a further misunderstanding. He could not come out at the other man. A friend regarded this, not as oversensitivity or unkindness, but as a *physical* inability to know how to break down the barrier. For weeks he did not speak to a close friend, though they met every day, until the other wondered what had gone wrong; and finally Newman wrote him a letter, to send his blessing, and to tell him that he wrote because he so often looked across at him at the time of recreation, hunting for something to talk about.

Then something in the stance was moral: the peril of words. Quite early in life he acquired a little fear of small talk. In his experience it easily turned empty, or malicious. It led into talk for the sake of sounding clever. Sometimes it led to theological debate where men discussed sacred things as though they were not sacred. He never lost this little fear of conversation. He once said, startlingly, and as a moral exhortation, 'Let us avoid talking, of whatever kind' (P 5.45).

Something in the stance was the feeling, how poor are words in this corrupt world. We have real feelings. Words prevent us from explaining the reality of these feelings; so we appear cold to one another when we are not.

He was conscious of being alone, not lonely. He was far more aware of being separate from his fellow-men than of being a member of human society. He thinks of Adam in his garden, just one human in the world, and in that very solitude Newman found something perfectly innocent, perfectly happy. When he looked down at a baby, he saw it as dependent, and yet withdrawn from its fellow-humans, unable to understand or communicate, fenced off from the world like Adam in his garden. When he looked at passers-by hurrying on the pavement, he could eye them with the feeling that each was the centre of his own universe, and behind each skin lay a depth unfathomable. He marvelled at the uniqueness of the individual, millions of humanity, everyone different, as though each flower had a special fragrance of its own.

Though this was a great churchman, who revived men's understanding of the essence of a Church, he was a solitary by intelligence; a friend but not sociable; one who had compassion for the people and yet was no man for the multitude. 'If we be in a crowd,' he once said, 'still be we as hermits in the wilderness' (P 5.115). The truest life is alone. He would think of the solitary man, able to bear his own company, and to take pleasure in it, for that is the grace of God within him. He would quote the old saying *Never less alone than when alone* (P 5.70). He was aware of a deep peace in the life of faith; never on the surface; unseen by the world, 'like some well in a retired and shady place, difficult of access' (P 5.69).

He saw society as full of pomp; its ritual forms, its empty ceremonies. He had a sympathy for the young, who react against the conventions of the world, and once compared true Christians to such rebels. This had a little kinship with his own withdrawal; the dingy cassock up against the immaculate cravats of a successful age. In 1872 an officious verger turned him out of St Paul's Cathedral, partly because he looked shabby. (It was his 'new' coat but had hung in his cupboard unused for a long time.) He did not mind.

He knew that part of his retirement, perhaps the main part, was not self-sacrifice but pleasure. 'I like going on my own way ... living without pomp or state, or pressing engagements. Put me into official garb and I am worth nothing; leave me to myself, and every now and then I shall do something' (L 24.213).

He loved the monotony of life in community. He thought of his room or cell as a nest from which he disliked to come. He devoted much of his day to writing – hence the vast collection of private letters. He thought on paper.

Behind the restrained or severe façade was an abundant demonstrative man. The hero in one of his novels kissed the willow-trees which he loved. Newman kissed the letter 'rapturously' which told him that a friend was elected a Fellow of Oriel College. His professions of friendship could sound like an excess. From his coach arriving in Rome he walked across the city barefoot to say his prayers in St Peter's. When he left Littlemore finally he kissed the bed and the mantlepiece and other parts of the house. When a ship, carrying supplies for soldiers in the Crimea, was sunk in a storm, he burst into tears as he read the newspaper. When a close friend died he sobbed bitterly over the coffin. When he revisited Littlemore nearly a quarter of a century after he left it, an Anglican clergyman recognised him and begged him to visit an old friend now bedridden; and Newman burst into tears and cried *Oh no Oh no!* but then went.

That none of this should be allowed into his religion is the more remarkable. He distrusted the unrestrained emotional language of evangelical pietism or popular Catholic superstition. He disliked the too plain appeal to feeling. Like all the old English high churchmen he inherited the fear of *enthusiasm*, and shrank from excitement in religion, and thought feverishness to be a sign of error.

Those who saw Newman at the sacrament were conscious that he was much with God. But he prayed in his own way. He had a lively mind and could not usually rest in long silences. He needed a lot of material for his prayers, a lot of thinking about Biblical texts or devotional authors. The mode was unusual. He thought best with pen and paper, and prayer was no exception. He formed sentences, drafted poetic aspirations, and channelled the mind to express a facet of faith or hope. The devotional books which he used were seldom classics. Almost anything served, especially if it were given him by a friend. We might expect such a man to enjoy prayer. But this was so only at moments; he suffered easily from feelings of aridity, and found prayer more often a duty than a pleasure. And he suspected that pleasure might bring with it less useful feelings, like pride in devotion, or excitement, or sense of abnormality; whereas prayer ought to be normal, sober, quiet, calm. Newman was no man for wordless silence or sudden outbreaks of emotion. He needed, and taught the need of, forms, regular words, short, simple, easy to use and never so elaborate that they overoccupy the mind or tempt it into formality. He loved, and revived the use of, the Private Prayers of Lancelot Andrews, bishop in the earlier seventeenth century; and these are a chain of scriptural phrases, no less original in their harmony because they are not the words of the bishop but his arrangement, and no less profound because they are staccato and hardly ever have a sentence more than a few words long. Newman once defined his own ideal thus: 'the lowliest, awfullest, calmest, concisest language we can' (P 4.227).

This restraint in Newman disappointed. Could he have led us into the secrets of the universe, and all he does is to tell us to be regular in familiar phrases? He was a poet. But he feared the unreality of an excess of poetry. We write about the mysteries of creation, and our language exalts our minds, and we come almost to think ourselves exalted — and is it real?

Within these solitary moods he suffered melancholies. In bad times he felt upon the edge of nothingness. This was the sensation which made the power in the most moving of all his verse, one of the enduring poems of Christian literature, *The Dream of Gerontius* (1865). Here a soul approached the brink of death, chill at heart, with a sense of abandonment, and emptying of being, and dropping into a shapeless abyss, and horror, and an infinite falling through a vacuum, his only hope in the prayers of his friends and of the saints. And then the soul struggled through to an act of faith, and acceptance of pain and fear, and at last to share in the adoration of the heavenly host; and so was escorted across the river to be purged, and put aside his fear, and found peace, and heard the angels singing a song like the summer wind among the pine trees; and the words came in an echoing refrain:

> Praise to the holiest in the height,
>   And in the depth be praise:
> In all His words most wonderful,
>   Most sure in all his ways . . .
> And that a higher gift than grace
>   Should flesh and blood refine,
> God's presence and his very self
>   And Essence all divine.

Newman, who loved theology because it was about God, and dismissed theological logic because it was not about God, would have smiled at the debate over the last verse, in what sense *presence* is a higher gift than *grace*.

These moods or melancholies were reflected in his letters. When he felt them heavy upon him, he wrote about them to his friends. The worst waves of melancholy hit his mind in his fifties and early sixties and again in his late seventies; but those were not the only black times. We need to beware against taking these fits of depression as normal in his life. When he was cheerful he seldom wrote it down, when he felt moody he relieved his sensations by sharing them on paper.

This then was a man withdrawn from the world; and with that withdrawal, a lone mind. In his twenties he was still to be influenced by Oxford colleagues and friends. By the time he passed the age of thirty-five he had become the solitary thinker. His ideas developed under his own meditation. He read many books, and thought about them much, and on occasion discussed them. But his mind was always his own. The Roman Catholics sent him to Rome to learn the laws of scholastic thought as taught by the tidiest schoolman of that day, Giovanni Perrone. Newman sat on the benches like a schoolboy, meek and teachable. He took into his mind almost nothing. Perrone respected Newman and thought him dangerous, Newman respected Perrone and thought him dry. The contrast between these two thinkers was as wide as possible. A poet versus the most prosaic of minds; a flowing fruitful pen versus a pen which is a filing system; boldness versus sensible adherence to tradition; a non-schoolman versus an archetypal schoolman; a man of the conscience versus a man of logic; an Oxford don versus a learned seminarist; and finally a budding Oratorian versus a Jesuit — the two minds were so far apart that we need to postulate special acts of grace to explain how they came to feel mutual respect.

Solitary thinkers are less easy to follow than philosophers of accepted schools. Readers or hearers wondered what he meant, asked whether the obvious implications were intended, panted and puffed, and quite often — especially when they were guardians of orthodoxy whether Protestant or Catholic — were disturbed and shocked. If they were shocked, their minions wrote nasty little notes in newspapers. While he was a Protestant, tutors and heads and bishops pored over his words to decide whether they were unfitting for a loyal English clergyman. While he was a Roman Catholic, censors at Rome pored over his words to decide whether they were heretical, or offensive to pious ears, or imprudent, or merely unfitting for a loyal priest. His mental processes were all his own, and he did not care if he startled.

During the only time when he had intellectual equals in his community — the years at Oriel College, especially the earlier years — he learnt much through academic duels and more by intellectual osmosis. Of this osmosis, far the most important source was the sweet-natured godly pastor and poet John Keble.

The withdrawal to a monastery was also a withdrawal to a mental hermitage. Neither Littlemore nor Birmingham were groups of scholar-monks. These were pastors, and confessors, and men of prayer, and teachers in school. No other mind in those communities compared with Newman's. That was a loss. He meditated, and drafted, and tore up, and meditated again. He did not hammer out his opinions under the scrutiny of an intellectual peer.

This gives the reader of Newman, at times, the impression that the mind is *enclosed*. Not *narrow*; it is too well-read; too original, too bold. But anyone who watches Newman make strange modern inferences from a study of the Monophysites of the fifth century, or examines his rage about a misguided plan to put a bishop into Jerusalem, realises that the solitary outlook has girt the mind with a hardly visible zariba. Not quite everything was seen in proportion.

Intellectual diffidence

He did not think much of himself as a thinker. One of the most edifying, even heroic, moments of Newman's life came when he sat on the benches in Rome during his second training for the priesthood. On all the things that he cared about, most of the things that mattered, he understood far better than the lecturers what was important in the modern world. He showed no sign of resentment, hardly a sign even of impatience. He fancied that he had a lot to learn.

This humble attitude to his own mind issued in odd uses of time. He took weeks off to do work extraordinary in so funda-mental a thinker. He wrote a couple of novels, neither of them good, both worth reading only for the author. He spent hours on schoolboy texts of Latin plays. When he came to write lasting works of divinity he behaved strangely. He made them sound very tentative; which is what he felt them to be.

The great French student of the spiritual life, Henri Bremond, said of Newman that among his intellectual equals he had the least enquiring mind of the last century. This is a very unjust verdict. Newman's mind always pushed against the edges of knowledge. The truth underlying the accusation is better expressed thus: he had so profound a sense of the mysteries of the universe that he was sceptical of anyone's success in probing. A man's mind may come to shadows of truth, and probabilities, and sudden poetic flashes of insight. Little purpose in toiling away to build a tower of the intellect which will only cramp reality and imprison truth so that it is no longer truth. His diffidence about himself kept thrusting itself into his intellectual processes. He conceived his mental endeavours as like struggles to get into a labyrinth, or to find the weak point in the battlements of a fortress — and not only struggles, almost always baffled struggles: the keep was near-impregnable. His mind had a knife. He knew very well that this knife was sharp. The edge was made no blunter by his devotions or his respect for authority. Yet the awareness of this property brought him no pride, and diminished not one whit his distrust of his mind. To possess a surgical instrument is not useful to the besieger of a bastion.

He could not bear to be treated as an oracle, or a holy man, or a sage. He had a hatred of all personal inflation as unreal.

The strangest of all signs of this self-distrust came during the years of convertitis after 9 October 1845. The mobs of Britain were out against Catholics. They were afraid of cheap Irish labour, and therefore they knew nothing and believed everything. For several months of 1850—1 the Oratorians might risk bricks if they went out into the streets. With this mass of heat and stupidity Newman could play delightful games, sometimes mocking gently, sometimes cleansing, sometimes enchanting; and could play less delightful games with the counter-prejudice of the convert, even with a savaging pen. This is a rare juxtaposition; a refined mind bothering itself with trash like *Maria Monk*, fables not worth any man's attention if they were not cited on the dais in the town hall at Birmingham. The reader laughs, and is sad to see so delicate an instrument taking its time to prove false what no instructed person could believe true. You feel that a skilled surgeon at a London hospital, whose time is precious for research and advanced operations, volunteered for months of his life to bandage chilblains at the local primary school. He bandages with panache, and everyone enjoys his services. Yet you cannot help a doubt whether this should be his vocation. No one could spend all that time destroying the reputation of a worthless Italian ex-friar like Achilli, unless he had a lowly opinion of his qualification for contributing to the study of the divine.

3 The reality of the Christian life

The religion of the Bible, as it was understood and practised by evangelical Protestants of England in the early nineteenth century, had doctrines. But it was not a cold system of dogma. They had a vivid sense of God's providence in the history of the world, and his care for the unique fate of each member of the human race. They felt themselves to be a chosen people, men and women with a vocation to serve God in the world. They had family prayers in their homes, and liked their young to be taught to read in their Bibles, and to know well their Biblical histories, and to be able to answer questions even on the obscure characters of old Hebrew history. They taught a high standard of behaviour in unselfishness and good manners and church-going. Their religion was as much of the house as of the church, as much private as public. They were seldom teetotallers. If a child had a talent for music, or art, or scholarship, he was encouraged and not repressed. Though they had more than a touch of the old puritan, they were not afraid of earning good money and used it to live in comfort without ostentation.

A schoolmaster at the Ealing boarding-school introduced Newman to the books of the Calvinists. The year was 1816, when the boy was fifteen years old.

Calvin's mind stood at the base of that interpretation of St Paul which marked all this school of religion. The boy Newman learnt how from all eternity God chose his soul for its calling; how the world was a warfare between heaven and hell, the city of light versus the city of everlasting night; that Christ by his sacrifice on the cross saved him from the powers of hell; and that faith in Christ issued in power to do right. He learned no rigid Calvinism. The sternest of the school supposed that from all eternity God destined some men to eternal torment. Newman had too broad an education, and neither his home nor his books accepted a doctrine which made God cruel. But he grew up a puritan, in modern English terms of that day an evangelical. He began to discipline his private life strictly.

After a time as an undergraduate at Trinity College, Oxford, he won a Fellowship at Oriel College. There he soon grew out of the puritanism of his schooldays; or rather, grew in mind, taking the puritanism with him, but understanding it in new ways, and seeing it now as part of a wider heritage within the tradition of Christendom.

To the vicarage of the University church of St Mary, opposite Oriel College, the College had the right of appointment. It always chose one of its Fellows. When Newman was only twenty-seven, the College made him the vicar of St Mary's. Though so young, he had position, a famous pulpit.

The sermons at St Mary's, Oxford, were the most important publication, not only of his Protestant days, but of his life: first volume 1834, six volumes in all. They were preached in the university church, but were parish sermons, not sermons to the University. The church had few parishioners in Oxford, and they not likely to understand what he said; the real parish lay out to the south-east at Littlemore, where he caused a little church to be built. Therefore the number of listeners at these sermons might be small, at times even a handful. He had not the arts of a popular preacher, and if he had those arts he shrank from using them. He read his sermons from behind a high lectern. The voice could be monotonous though it was also musical, and the impact, when it made impact, was not of fire but of sincerity. Some could not understand, and some fell asleep. But slowly the special gifts came clear to a growing group of sensitive Oxford minds, whether of undergraduates or senior members. The man was teaching them about Christian truth in a way which they had not heard before, and commanded beauty of prose-poetry as a fitting vehicle for his thought. As he grew famous, Oxford tutors started devices for discouraging young men from going to hear, and so encouraged them to go.

The six volumes of *Parochial and Plain Sermons* make a corpus of writing which, with the volume of University Sermons from the same years, are Newman's chief work. He never wrote better; never more powerfully, never more persuasively. These books of sermons made the heart of that body of thought which came in history to be known as the Mind of the Oxford Movement.

The *Parochial Sermons* are severe; in bulk as severe a corpus of sermons as were ever preached. He sees through everything. You feel penitent – you are at least half pretending before God. You say you have repented – empty word, repentance is a life-long growth. You look back with gratitude, but if you were aware of God, you would look back with fear. You love hymns and delude yourself that this makes you religious, and perhaps you are a man of sentiment and not of religion.

The power in the sermons is at bottom the quest for reality in religion. The eighteenth century used a lot of religious language that was sacrificial, and was comfortable in not practising what it preached. The Victorians saw the hypocrisy. And though they confessed the eternal gap between effort and success, they were determined that the gap should be seen for what it was, and that Christians should realise a never-ending discontent with themselves. This would have happened without Newman. But Newman came into the pulpit just when people felt the discontent but had not quite expressed it. He articulated what they felt, drove it home, and spread the discontent to an ever-widening circle of minds. This was what led some of his followers to ascribe vast consequences to his words, and to believe that he altered the entire feeling among the English people towards religion.

He had a programme, pursued steadily week by week, and volume by volume. He aimed at an extraordinary goal, which in another man might have seemed absurd or overweening: no less than to raise the standard of religious practice. He read deeply in the early Christian Fathers and the classical Anglican divines of the later Reformation. He looked out upon the Church around him, and contrasted it with what he found in the past, and saw a thin formality in religion, dry prayers drily recited by a dry clerk before a dumb congregation, sermons that were moral platitudes, sacraments that were treated as empty of grace. Or at the other extreme he saw crude revivalism, ignorant and unctuous and tasteless. He exaggerated the defects of what he saw. He counted too little of the strength in family religion, of the force for good in the congregational hymn, of the popular magnetism of the evangelical preachers. But overstating or not, he saw the need to recall the Church to its own principles: a sacramental life, a way of self-sacrifice, a richer treasure-house of doctrine and prayer.

Therefore the sermons sometimes exaggerate. His revulsion was absolute, his demand excessive, his dogma harsh. And yet he was always able to be lofty without being pretentious, and to condemn whatever was small or shallow without sounding arrogant. R. W. Church, who listened to him week by week for several years, said of him, 'he placed the heights of religion very high'.

His doctrine was the doctrine of the old high Anglican Fathers, before the revolution of 1688. The novelty that he preached was only novel to his time. But the context was novel. He had a sense of the rich resources in the meditation by the Church on the Bible. He set the Prayer Book of the Church of England in a broader setting of a centuries-long devotion; and as he did so, showed how this was not archaic nor antiquarian nor donnish, but mattered to everyone in a pew; how creeds of long-dead bishops expressed a living faith which now passed to their heirs. He realised that a creed was not to be apprehended by intellectual surgery, but was part of a way of worship, and to be seized within the immeasurable mysteries of the universe, and directed to men who walk in the land of shadows and reflections, to bring light and truth enough for their journey amid a landscape with limitless horizons.

In this way, though the sermons are full of doctrine, the doctrine is never cold. It is surrounded by a halo of awe, never separated from a moral aim, and always practical in its consequences.

He was intensely conscious of the other world. At times he was so aware of the inward reality that the outer circumstances of life began to seem cloud-castles; and there were moments when this sensation grew so strong as to lead him into thoughts hard to reconcile with Christianity; of life as 'a sort of dream, as detached and as different from our real eternal existence as a dream differs from waking', 'a scene set before us in which we seem to be'; language more akin to Plato than to the New Testament. He imagined the soul at its best sitting by a shady quiet well of water where few come; happy in the company of an eternal comforter, not missing the conversation of the talkative, wanting nothing, and not caring if away in the city men say hard things about his retreat (P 4.221–7).

Men who dare to preach sincerity are spotted at the first breath of insincerity. Newman felt called to the task; was convinced of the truth of what he said; had a manner that sounded dry or flat to the uninitiated, but was magnetic to those who fell under his spell; understood the moral and personal predicaments of the human race; was unlike most of the preachers of his day in having no tricks, no inflation of words, nothing artificial; and commanded a simple style which was the perfect instrument in language for what he needed to say.

It was warmth rather than fire. Always there was restraint. The language was moderate, the mood calm; he never sought to convert by excitement. He never sparkled. He never ceased to appeal to the head in his probing of the heart. Sensible men found a preacher who said sensible things which, unlike most sensible sermons, touched their emotions. The more overwhelming the reality, the more the preacher's personality started to hide. Popular preachers create their effect by making their personality large. Newman created his effect by disappearing into the reality of which he spoke, as though he must get out of its way.

More than one of his disciples reported another quality. He took a single theme and went after it as a seeker; not with doubt, nor with the labour that tires, but with a steady pushing into the mysteries at the centre of his subject. He seemed to one listener to be like an eagle swooping unerringly upon its prey. He might lead the hearers into mystery; he never lost his consciousness that the universe is a very mysterious place and that mortal mind can only touch its fringes; but he never left his audience muddled by mystery, or confused about what they heard.

Everyone is agreed that he was not an 'orator'; that his strength lay partly in not being an 'orator'; and yet that the effect of his words could be as piercing as the highest flights of a Bossuet. If true oratory is to use words so that they please and move, then Newman was an orator. The critics did not like to think of him as an orator because of his plainness of speech. Yet his disciples are agreed that in the simplicity there could be heard music; and that this music did not depend solely upon the timbre of the voice, nor on magic in the manner, but came directly out of the words which he used and the coherence of his personal attitude with those words.

This is the preacher for the Industrial Revolution. These were the times when new machines produced new goods for the consumer; the years when the chance of wealth could be seen, and the pursuit of wealth could be magnetic; of new luxury and new materialism, and new pleasure in possession, and new desire to rise in society. In the middle of all this Newman stood for rejection of wealth as an end, or rising in class as a way to happiness. He is the prophet of self-denial in the world of growing material comfort, and his cry for self-denial can be brutal.

He never ceased to think, and never ceased to remind, that the prophets wore sheepskins and goatskins, that John the Baptist ate the food of the wilderness, that Christ had nowhere to lay his head, and that in the Gospel all the luxurious men are uncomfortable.

These are the sermons of a young man. The difficulty of preaching consists not in making a sermon but afterwards, in doing what one said. Wise men dare not preach too strongly lest they tell others to do what they know they will never do themselves. Only young people dare preach fasting to the limit because only young stomachs bear fasting to the limit. Still in his thirties, Newman could watch, and pray, and meditate, and deny himself, and be rigorous in his private austerity.

Pastors of sixty rummage among their old sermons preached thirty years before, and are disturbed at their presumption, or sad that the years lowered their standards instead of fostering their growth. They rue that now they would not dare to say what once they said with sincerity. The reason for this is not only sin. It is a livelier sense of the possible.

Not so Newman. In the strength of his earlier years he did not shrink from the strongest words; and his disciples saw that his endeavour was consistent with those words. Decades afterwards, in his later sixties, he did not hesitate to republish. Experience taught him what as a young vicar he never quite realised, that not even all dedicated men and women ought to aspire to heroism. Nevertheless the aged cardinal saw nothing too fierce in the words of the young Newman.

He studied — more than studied, he revered the age of the early Christians. In his eyes this was catholicity, and his ideal of the Church.

From the time that he was a young Oxford don he dedicated himself to raising the Church to accept its full inheritance of catholicity. Partly by lapse of time and partly by the weakness of men, there came incongruity between catholicity and the average English Protestantism of 1830. Newman aimed to screw the second up to the first. He was a true reformer.

Once he drew a portrait of a true reformer. To be a reformer you need zeal, even aggression. Yet you are never to lose gentleness. You are not to identify the movement with God's cause in the sense of believing that all opponents must be wicked. You must have a single eye set upon the goal. You must never despise, either the people who attack or the people whom you try to reform.

He wanted all sorts of practical things: boards taken down from over altars; the abolition of taking money at the doors; fonts not used as stands for hats; churches unlocked when it was not time for service; tearing away of filthy cloths; sweeping out the air of damp and neglect that might be found in many country churches; an end to vestry-meetings inside churches; an end to preferring sermons to sacraments; driving orchestras out of sanctuaries; an end to the right by which infidels could appoint to church offices.

He wanted to bring back reverence. He saw people come into church, gossip, look about, use the kneeler not for their knees but for their feet, lounge, treat the church as more like a hall than a house of God, be funny or caustic about the sermon. He hated men to be 'free and easy' in church. They come into a Presence before whom even the seraphim veil their faces. Men treat God as an appendage to their feelings of self-satisfaction and truly they should feel self-abasement. We are not to make services exciting, nor use florid oratory in the pulpit, nor crack jokes to entertain. We shall be grave, and quiet, and care nothing if the superficial say that sobriety is dull. We shall be sure that our outward forms are reverent — dress for the minister, kneeling to confess, an ordering of the body and its posture. And we shall be sure that these forms are not for-malities, but the outward expression of awe within the soul.

He cared little about ritual, and yet he cared much. As he retained simplicity of dress or furniture in his private life, and thought it sin and bad taste to do otherwise, so in his chapel he kept furnishing and behaviour to an old austerity. He called mere ritualists 'gilt-gingerbread' men (A 422).

And yet we can see why later Anglo-Catholics wanted more elaborate ritual and could not think that they disobeyed Newman. External show, he was sure, we must suspect. But due external order we need, for man worships, and man is body as well as soul.

These sermons are not personal in any improper sense. The pronoun *I* is not used beyond necessity. Yet the kind of man preaching comes through.

He is a man with a conviction of providential care; of the hand of God leading him in his private life, understanding him with compassion, choosing him to be his servant; with a con-sciousness that from time to time his prayers have been answered even if he cannot say when; with a sense of mysterious forces about him. Before the unknown quality in the world he has awe, before its vastness and its refusal to fit men's definitions. He is a man who does not find it strange that the very hairs of our head are numbered. He finds in his faith the key to unlock the secrets of the universe; and thinks that those who cannot share this faith roam amid the shadows and interpret things at random.

He is a man conscious that any way forward is a groping, whether morally or in the mind. You are in the dark. You bump about into objects, often the objects which you never meant to bump. Because you recognise error you are a little less far from the truth. So with moral growth. You fail; and the failure is the ground of penitence. Mostly we choose not between two right acts but whichever is less wrong. 'We walk to heaven backward; we drive our arrows at a mark, and think him most skilful whose shortcomings are the least' (P 5.108).

He is a man with a quick anxious conscience, who feels the pricks of guilt like physical pain.

He hates it when men take God's name casually; or when they argue about such an idea as the Holy Trinity as though they argue about a theory of science or a doubt of history; or when they declare with certainty that they are saved; or when they despise other men's reverent acts; or when they address God in prayer with terms of endearment; or when they pretend to address God in prayer, but use such rolling periods and pompous manner that they evidently mean to address their hearers; or when they pretend to pray by external posture but do not pray; or peer all about a church with inquisitiveness, forgetful of why they came.

He is an intelligent man who knows that the conscience does more for truth than the intelligence; an eloquent man who fears oratory; a subtle logician with the lowest opinion of logic; a fertile mind with small regard for originality; a thinker who despises the idea of speculation; a reasoner who wants reason valued in its proper place but that place lowly in the order of creation. These six volumes make one of the great English works of moral divinity. They are not so recognised. The Roman Catholic saw them as a Protestant work. The Anglican saw them as vitiated because their author deserted the cause. What happened in 1845 diminished for nearly three decades the number of their readers and for several more decades the respect with which they were read. But more than a century and a half later we can forget the scruples and take them for what they are: a corpus of writing which stands comparison with a classic of the seventeenth century like Jeremy Taylor.

4 Faith

The origins of faith

Newman was a man in whom the memory of his childhood roused feelings of reverence and affection. It carried in his recollection more than a touch of nostalgia, and an aura of tenderness. He felt this most at Christmas. He could remember, or believed that he could remember, how as a child he had a pure discernment of the existence of an unseen world, and a 'realization of what is Sovereign and Adorable'. He did not idealise children. But as he looked at them, he thought how they came lately from the hand of God; and he revered the simplicity of their ways, the artlessness, the ignorance of evil, the confession of helplessness, above all the sense of wonder.

The baby's first realisation is dependence. The only need is bodily: milk, comfort. As a child grows, life is found to be more than bodily comfort. There comes self-knowledge, distinctness, individuality. At first it is enough that things can be made to obey. But little by little even things are not enough. If the heart rests in things, it will be disappointed. Within is discomfort, a craving for something unknown but higher; and at last the soul is perceived as independent of things – something in humanity is more lasting than things. And if the material world grows changeable, or misfortune befalls, the soul is set amid a world that by comparison falls away towards nothing. Thus the human child rises towards the permanence beyond the world. The physical world becomes a veil, thick but not so thick that it altogether hides what is beyond; and at last comes spirit with spirit – God on one side, the soul on the other; rising to the perception that 'there are but two beings in the whole universe, our own soul, and the God who made it' (P 1.20).

We long to penetrate this veil. We want truth, and permanence, and lasting happiness. But this world is very visible; a very opaque screen between our eyes and what we know to be there but cannot see.

We find that, in seeking to penetrate this veil, to look outwards is useless. Experience shows that to look outwards always meets an impenetrable barrier of cloud. Conventional wisdom in the first half of the nineteenth century said that wonderful designs in nature proved a Designer; that we need only look upon the beetle's wing or the human retina to see design; that if we look upward to sun and moon and stars, we see the mathematical beauty of an infinite design. Newman believed none of this. Experience shows that the only way is to look within. 'I believe in design because I believe in God, not in a God because I see design.' A future bishop, who disliked the scepticism about the intelligence, once pressed him with the words of a woman who said that some people were certain of the Christian religion because they had proved it strictly. Newman gave a laconic answer. 'No one is certain for this reason' (L 25.97, 324).

Therefore look not outward but within. By examining the soul and its nature, we begin to discern reflections from beyond the veil. 'Self-knowledge is at the root of all real religious knowledge' (P 1.42). And this is why the beginning of true religion cannot lie in a book, or in science, or in arguing, or in listening to sermons. To look into the soul is to begin to find God. However able the sermon, however sacred the book, it will teach nothing to the person who has not started to look inward. The words of the Bible, the lessons of the Church, might draw the eye to look inward. But even they will teach nothing unless the eye looks inward.

For if we look inward we find conscience. We understand what sin is. We find a law which is not the law made by society. It is an ultimate law. And we find that disobedience to this law stirs feelings of guilt.

Light from beyond

Conscience says, you must obey this moral law. Where does that law come from? Who gave the order? Nobody in this world ordered what my conscience feels a call to obey. This law, by

existing, proves that in the universe there is something beyond
the barrier of sense. No one can live without acting as though
something in the world is not material but spiritual. Something
or Someone is beyond the veil.

We look round at our fellows. We see that many of them
record messages, or light, from beyond the veil. They are agreed
in finding a link between this light and their moral duty. They
see the *moral* law as never to be separated from the gift of
religious truth. They talk of light, faint or fragmentary, but
enough for the purpose of moral conviction; and, however faint
or fragmentary, so powerful in its moral force that you can
hardly fail to receive it if you keep your eyes open.

These rays from beyond the veil are 'given'. That is, the
reason does not seek them out. The whole person, of which the
reason is the thinking guide, is conscious of light coming. But
the reason does not seek to discover whether it is of this kind or
that, other than by the certainty, deeper than reason, that the
purpose of the light from beyond the veil is moral. The light is
not given to satisfy our minds. It is not given to make the world
look tidy. It is given to make us better men.

The growth of faith

We live a material life. Something in us knows, and we cannot
be mistaken, that matter is not the only part of life. Inside us we
find a whisper, even a voice, or at least the echo of a voice, to
tell that something is higher than the earth. We cannot analyse
or define this voice. It prompts us to religion, it rebukes sin. It is
a yearning in our nature. But this yearning 'is met and sus-
tained, it finds an object to rest upon, when it hears of the
existence of an all-powerful, all-gracious Creator' (P 6.340).
The source of the ultimate law must be 'personal'. We do not
feel shame before a horse. The sense of conscience is only to be
explained by a relation to a law that is beyond humanity and yet
is 'intelligent'.

We find that Church and Bible speak to us of this law. We
discover harmony between what we find in ourselves and the
evidence given by religious souls.

The Bible gave mankind a message. This message needs understanding, and interpreting. To interpret needs right reason. But when is reason right? It is not a machine in the head, leaving the rest of the person behind. Its rightful use depends on an inward attitude in the user. Part of this attitude is a harmony between the mind which interprets and the Bible which is being interpreted. And this harmony is not mainly intellectual, though it is indeed a sympathy of the intelligence. At bottom it is moral. To understand the Bible the soul begins with very simple truths, such as a child perceives. These truths touch the conscience. Slowly the conscience grows in sensitivity and perception. And as the conscience becomes aware, so the reason sees a new range and depth in the truths which it seeks to understand.

Moral growth is the condition of the right understanding of the Bible. Without moral growth no right understanding is possible. The soul sees a simple truth. Then the conscience is touched, and looks upward. As it looks, and moves, grace touches the mind and leads it into a new truth, or a deeper perception of the truth that at first was so simple and remains at bottom simple.

But here the soul is not alone. From the apostles came the Church, with its prayers, and its way of worship, and creed, and manner of life. In this community the soul finds the simple truths, framed as a rule of faith. We do not go to the Bible and there learn a creed. We come into the Christian community, learn the simplest truths of the creed, and so are led to the Bible. The community takes us to the Bible, not the Bible to the community; though, as we understand more about the Bible, we understand more about the community. The surest way to misunderstand the Bible is to attempt the feat as a mind not already within the Christian way of life.

This moral way towards truth is the reason why Christian teachers were always 'reserved' in the imparting of the gospel. The newcomer is capable only of receiving 'rudiments'. This is not because the brain is stupid – this new convert may be of supreme intellect. Let the soul grow in grace, and in sensitivity of conscience; then the mind will be able to receive more. Therefore the Christian teacher leads a mind onward and upward, as it is capable of receiving. The Church does not throw the most sacred truths, of oneness with God, or of sacramental grace, at the heads of converts just coming out of pagan axioms and morals. It withholds, because it knows that such cannot rightly be apprehended until the new disciple has come along the Christian way.

A religious idea does not need to be fully conscious, or expressed in conscious language. A person may hold a truth yet not know how to express that truth. Poets are hardly conscious of all that readers and critics find in their poetry. Autobiographers know that slowly they came to hold such and such opinions but have the sorest difficulty in saying quite how or when. Knowledge may be *inward* without being put into words. And yet that inward knowledge can be not only real but lasting. Quite often we read a book and *recognise* what we thought. We say, this is how I thought all the time but had not been able to express myself. A soul is led onward and comes to contemplate a light which is a ray of truth yet hardly capable of being expressed in words. Then, as the mind contemplates, it will try to put into words what is felt; but the words will be poetical, symbolic, reflecting rather than pointing. The eye is content with glimpses of what is too great for ordinary language. But as the soul is part of the Christian community, others have passed this way before; and left for our use a treasure of poetry, in psalms and hymns and meditations. This language will become part of the mental structure. Through it the soul will share in devotions far richer than the meagre phrases of a single mind.

The experience of the Church

The Church prays in its public worship. The individual prays, sometimes cannot do other than pray. Private prayer may be in any words. But — because we can never express for ourselves what we feel in worship — we should use the forms set by the Church even in private prayer. Prayers framed at the moment are often irreverent in expression. We cannot frame words adequately. The Church cannot frame the words fully. But its words will be less poor because moulded and sifted in the experience of generations. Such forms should always be sober in tone, never excited nor emotional. They should be short.

The soul can never outgrow these forms of prayer. The reason is this: the deeper the mystery of God is penetrated, the more impossible to express the experience in language. However near to God, the mind will still need formulas, put into the mouth by the Church.

Religious truth is not to be accepted with the top of the head, like a calculation of the width of the English Channel. The community has to live this truth. Its members meditate on it, dwell on it, draw out its meaning, apply it in moral predicaments, come to an affection for it, learn to give it reverence.

In this way a 'dogma' is not a bald, hard, literal sentence. It is a mode of expression which can only be understood rightly in relation to a surrounding of religious life and experience; and it is by leading that religious life that we come to understand the 'dogma' more fully. In this way a superficial enquirer can sometimes find one or more Christian 'dogmas' harsh or even repellent. The reason may be that moral attitudes are not right; or it may be that the words are taken out of their context, which is a whole world of moral endeavour and religious experience and spiritual insight. In the same way mere adherence to 'dogma' need not even be religious.

To look along the shelves of a great library moved Newman's heart as well as his head. If his eye ran along the spines of the books and saw great names – Clement, Origen, Tertullian, Cyprian, Augustine, Gregory, Leo, Basil and the others, all thinkers from the early years of Christianity – he saw each of them as a *trophy* (S 315), that is, a monument set up to the victories of the faith; this book is the record of a godly mind of past centuries, spending its eyes and its years, sacrificing comfort and family, to help ordinary men and women understand their faith better, and to make the Church conscious of its riches, moral and spiritual.

The divinity of the Church will never be a tidy system of thought. It cannot be a great articulated structure regular in shape. For it is built here a little and there a little. The gospel, being lived out, meets a new environment, new axioms of society, a new fashion in the schools, new discoveries in history, new scientific theories, controversies within the Church over the value of new-fangled phrases. We cannot expect an architect's palace in theology; but a house, rambling, strangely incomplete in certain directions, with outhouses built on at different epochs, a wing in one style next to a wing in a later and different style; but still a whole, consistent, harmonious, and all the more fascinating for its rambling.

Someone asks, how do you know the Bible comes from God? Then how should you answer? The philosopher's answer will be the same whether the questioner is a mocker, a heathen, or a Christian saint. But this was not Newman's way. He looks at the moral status of the enquiry. If the questioner is a mocker, say nothing. For that questioner has no chance whatever of understanding the reply. If this is a humble seeker after truth, then answer.

The little fragmentary texts of the New Testament are like keystones or foundations in the building. Without them it would tumble. Without them nothing lasting can be built.

By all such language we are still seeing through a glass darkly. The total thrust of all such words is reserved for a future, the sight of God in heaven. We are not given total truth. We are given enough light by which to live. But though we see through a glass darkly, we nevertheless see truth; sometimes inadequate, sometimes partial, sometimes vague, but still truth in the sense that the earthly idea reflects a little fragment of a reality beyond the veil.

Newman's violin entered this argument. He marvelled that out of so few notes and such few sounds composers could construct mighty harmonies, such symphonies and oratorios. We can analyse it, and describe it; and yet within it is a glory which we can only feel and cannot describe in any words which we would ourselves believe to be sufficient.

Can it be that those mysterious stirrings of heart, and

keen emotions, and strange yearnings after we know not what, and awful impressions from we know not whence, should be wrought in us by what is unsubstantial, and comes and goes, and begins and ends in itself? ... It cannot be ... They have escaped from some higher sphere; they are the out-pourings of eternal harmony in the medium of created sound; they are echoes from our Home; they are the voice of angels, or the Magnificat of saints, or the living laws of divine governance, or the divine attributes; something are they besides themselves, which we cannot compass, which we cannot utter – though mortal man, and he perhaps not other-wise distinguished above his fellows, has the gift of eliciting them'. (S 346)

Thus music is like the harmony, or rather the harmonies, of the Christian faith. That faith rests upon a few simplicities. These simplicities are reasoned upon, pondered, used in different contexts, until we meet structures of thought which never exhaust the realities which lie beneath.

Can you argue a man into faith? If you can argue him in you can argue him out. The faith of the simple is as certain as the faith of the educated. Therefore the grounds of faith cannot just be argument. To make argument the basis of faith is like trying to make a man religious by libraries or musicians. It is like taking a chemist for a cook.

But here enters philosophic doubt. Faith is certain of its object. Evidence can produce answers which are never more than probable. By what leap (if it is a leap) does the religious mind pass from the probable to the certain?

This problem was no easier for Newman because a dominant tradition in the divinity of both his Churches denied its basis. They taught that every sensible person, not blinded by immorality, can see reasons for certainty about the existence of God and so be led to the act of faith. Those who said that faith had secret grounds, or grounds not easily to be explained by argument, these schools were likely to anathematise.

This was Newman's supreme intellectual difficulty. Officialdom said that everyone who doubted, doubted because of sin. Newman knew that this sweeping condemnation was preposterous. Anything that he said on this subject would be suspect to the conventional. Yet he felt it as the ultimate problem of his day and needed to say something, if only to clear his own mind. He did not find it easy. 'Whenever I attempted, the sight I saw vanished, plunged into a thicket, curled itself up like a hedgehog, or changed colours like a chameleon' (L 25.199).

The human race cannot live in universal doubt. Not even philosophers are capable of this feat. We have to act. We cannot wait for a long chain of arguments before we act. The food may be poisoned. We know it is not, we trust the people, we have certainty based on trust. We are certain that we know which two persons are our parents. This certainty is based only on trust in people. We know not only that an act is right but why it is right. We see that the rightness of the act depends upon a far wider moral context. And in this certitude a mind is conditioned by all sorts of things — heredity, and upbringing, and experience, bearing upon a theme and finding the insight that leads to assurance of truth. And until this assurance comes, the person is not fully a person. Character only becomes character when not blown about by every wind of argument.

Some truth is certain, though to the philosopher only probable. A man who has never been to India would be a fool to doubt that India exists though strictly speaking he has only probability. We are certain that Britain is an island though we have not sailed round the coasts. In the same way only a corrupt mind could believe that all the religious experience reported by the human race is nothing but buzzing in the ears. Objective truth is presented to the intelligence. Faith is not mere feeling.

Yet the religious mind sees reasons where the irreligious does not. Personal opportunity, and a vision of a moral ideal, and a slow semi-conscious apprehension of the objectivity of God in the world, lie underneath the reasoning faculty; and the evidence which this growth provides is not available to all men alike. The nature of faith, regarded in its aspect of knowing, is far more akin to the knowledge of a person than to the knowledge of a scientific theory. An element of trust enters the knowledge. A man has affection for his wife. He has no duty to hesitate if he hears evidence that the sun is further away than scientists have commonly taught. If someone brings him evidence that his wife is unfaithful, he has a moral duty to hesitate because it contradicts all his experience of her, and that experience contains a trust in the future as well as a knowledge of the present.

The illative sense

The famous formula of Newman's last years is the phrase *illative sense*. He coined the expression to describe the act of assent in the mind based upon a body of grounds in their totality, even though the mind is not aware of all the grounds treated as separate arguments, and may be resting on half-inarticulate experience as well as argument. This was the assent which turned the accumulation of probabilities into certitude. This doctrine had consequences against the dominant theory of faith. 'While I can prove Christianity divine to my own satisfaction,' wrote Newman, 'I shall not be able to force it upon anyone else' (G 408).

No one else has ever taken the phrase *illative sense* into his jargon.

In understanding the theory two principles must always be borne in mind:

(1) when Newman wrote of certitude, he did not mean certain knowledge. He meant the conviction in a man's mind that he has certain knowledge.

(2) The ultimate principle is this: right moral attitudes foster right intellectual attitudes. This is at the bottom of the whole idea of *growing* through faith, into truth.

The distrust of 'mere' intellect

Newman discovered an alarming principle. He expressed it boldly: *Religious light is intellectual darkness* (P 1.211). This is one of the sayings which caused this intelligent man to be accused of hostility to the intelligence. He was charged with going even as far as the old Christian father who said, *I believe because it is absurd*.

But Newman's thought was much more delicate than that. The world is easy for philosophers so long as they ask none of the questions that count. If they confine themselves to matter they are only in difficulty if they manufacture difficulty. If they confine themselves to logic and meaning, they are in many difficulties which are not manufactured, but the area is a tiny corner of life. At the moment when they begin to ask great questions of traditional philosophy – of free will, and predestination, and providence, and purpose, and evil, and God – they are in darkness.

Then the moral being comes with the conscience and finds in religion light by which that conscience may live. This light does not diminish the philosopher's darkness. It is likely to increase it. Evil is no problem for the mind until it is seen as sin. Suffering is no problem for the mind until it is seen as part of a world that a good God made. The religious mind, however dimly, sees light. And the light is not so dim but that it displays itself as a ray from some more brilliant and mysterious entity still concealed. In this sense we must understand the phrase *Religious light is intellectual darkness*.

If you doubt God, the answer is not to debate whether He exists. It is to go and try to live according to that conscience which responds to the ultimate law which is found to be God's.

Newman was an intellectual who distrusted the intellect. This distrust remained with him all his life. But it was expressed in tougher language when he was young than when he was old. The reason lies partly in the boldness of youth versus the mellowness of age; partly because half-way through his course he met a lot of Roman thinkers who hated assailants of the intellect; and partly because the conflict between reason and faith was sharper to him in youth. In 1834 nearly everyone believed that Genesis was true in all its history. Since this was untrue, the strain on men's belief grew as each generation grew to manhood. Newman was better fitted than most Catholic thinkers (we shall see) to cope with this stress among the Churches; because when he spoke of doubt, the ultimate which must not be doubted was always the light of conscience within. But in the 1830s Christianity seemed to mean believing (among other things) that Balaam's ass talked in human speech with his master. And under such conditions — when faith looked to hang on absurdity — even Newman came near to saying, I believe although it is absurd. Therefore this distrust of the intellect was uttered more vehemently in his earlier years. He lost the vehemence, but never lost the distrust. He knew to the end that cleverness opens no gate to truths that matter.

Credulity?

What should be the attitude of the soul to light coming from beyond the veil? Evidently not critical. Not detached. Not neutral. For the light does not come like a piece of news to the head. It comes wrapped up with a command to the conscience. Perhaps the right attitude is *submission*; or, if that is too strong a word, *obedience*; or, if that is not the response of everyone, at least *readiness to receive*. That is, the link between the light coming, and the duty which it enlightens, makes us throw ourselves towards that light, expect to find it as a guide, receive it with hope and trust.

Experience shows that consciences may be mistaken about the light. They easily deceive themselves. They easily corrupt, easily squint, easily reflect it misshapen.

Newman asked a question which only he could ask. Which is better, to receive too much or to receive too little? If we are submissive to everything that comes our way we shall take what is false for what is true. We shall believe what no sensible man could ever believe. We shall be *credulous*. If we stay cold, and keep our distance, and analyse, and do a balancing act, and say *Yes it might be true*, we shall fail to take the most precious truths offered to our moral lives. Which is the worse danger, the danger of believing too much or the danger of believing too little? Can credulity ever be a good state of mind? — not good as an ideal, but good because less bad than the other course of diluting faith with so much worldly reason that it ceases to be the gift which came from beyond the veil?

Newman's answer to this question was hurled at his head by his enemies. He said openly that the 'credulous' was a more religious temper of mind than the 'sagacious' (P 2.20). We can well understand why the heads of Oxford colleges tried to stop their undergraduates from going to hear his sermons, when we meet such an utterance as this: 'It would be a gain to this country, were it vastly more superstitious, more bigoted, more . . . fierce in its religion, than at present it shows itself' (P 1.320). Is superstition then virtue? Not at all, it is sad error. Is bigotry then virtue? Bigotry is bad. Bigotry is Pharisaism. But we fail to realise that it is a perversion of virtues, namely zeal and reverence. Cold complacency seemed to Newman a worse sin than bigotry, which at least is hot for truth even if its eyes are blinkered.

As part of the charge that he encouraged credulity, men attacked him for excessive willingness to believe in miracles. He wrote two essays on miracles which were not likely to be admired by anyone who thought that common sense has something to do with sound religion. But when we examine what Newman says, we find that his underlying attitude is more critical than we might expect. The early Christians expected wonders and rejoiced in the immediacy of God. Since the earliest Christians were the truest Catholics, is it Catholic to rejoice in miracles?

Historical enquiry shows that some miracles were falsely reported, and never happened. We cannot rule out miracles solely on a previous axiom, *Miracles never happen*. God is sovereign. To that sovereign all things are possible. This is not to say that all things said to have happened have happened. We must set these mysteries within the mystery of the world; the strangeness amid the species of animals, the inexhaustible variety of nature, the exquisite subtlety of colouring, the marvellous diversity of instinct and passion. No one can ascribe to the world a pattern remorseless or material. If all the world is strange, God's acts may be to our eyes strange. The Lord gave a commission to the apostles, that they should heal. And in all ages the Church succeeds to the apostles and has witnessed such healing. In the Church is found an abiding presence; and, now here now there, this presence is felt or seen suddenly; 'gleams, shadows, traces of almighty power' (M 217).

Whether an event reported as miracle was miracle, that is another question. We fully expect in witnesses fiction or exaggeration. We can well believe most of the stories about the saints' miracles to be fables. But a wise judgement refuses to reject wonderful things where they are moral, or where they have parallels in experience, and at least holds the mind open and in suspense, and asks for light, and is always conscious that God is the sovereign of the world.

When Newman became a Roman Catholic his critics remembered the provocative language about credulity. Nor did they forget the essays on miracles. And his very first years as a Roman Catholic (1845–51), while he was suffering from convertitis, were the time of Newman's life when he was willing to believe, at least provisionally, what was incredible; like the story that Jesus's home at Nazareth was moved by angels to Loreto in North Italy. The new convert's mind was very submissive in his new Church; much more submissive than it later became when he recovered his balance.

In the theory of faith this was a real difficulty. Conscience leads you to God. God offers you a Church bearing truth about Himself. Reason now comes in to analyse the nature of the Church and the nature of the truth which it offers. But although reason comes in, it is 'reason-within-the-Church'. By the nature of the theory, ordinary scientific reasoning can have nothing to say, because science can never pass beyond the veil of sense. We can only ask which Church appears to us, as possessing a conscience and as historians, most faithful to its given origins.

The structure of the Church

This community in which we deepen faith has a structure: Christ – apostles – bishops – clergy – laity. This structure is given.

It is the way in which light from the other world is intended to be brought to mankind. From this structure any Christian is wrong to separate. Obedience to conscience comes soon to mean obedience to the Church.

Protestants were very suspicious about the idea of obeying the Church. They knew that they must always test the Church by the Bible. The most extraordinary thing – dare we say, the most miraculous thing? – about Newman was that he could persuade even devout Protestants to sing with heartfelt feeling such a verse as this:

> And I hold in veneration
> For the love of Him alone
> Holy Church as His creation
> And her teachings as His own.

The Church teaches simplest truths to the simple, and then leads them onward and upward through moral growth and the encouragement of a spiritual perception, to an ever deeper insight into the nature and object of faith. The Church is the Christian people. Therefore it comes to frame its faith better as time passes. Just as the single person starts with simple truths, so the Churches started with simple truths. Only as questions arose, and men used new devotional language, could the Church decide formally that such an expression or such a word was right.

The consensus of the faithful

In this way the Church has three organs of expression. First there are the bishops, especially (as Newman came to believe from 1843) the Pope, who are modern apostles and in council have the duty to declare and express the mind of the Church. Then there are theologians, whose work is necessary to the life of the Church, because they study the body of doctrine and devotion, and draw out the meaning, and perceive where conflicts may arise, and explain how this teaching is affected by new discoveries in history or new fashions in philosophy, and adapt the language to the needs of a new generation with a different kind of education and a different kind of moral crisis. And finally there are the people. These are not passive hearers, accepting what they are told. They are the repository of that profound understanding, hardly expressed in words, which is the Church's immediate apprehension of the Christian way of life. They are not theologians and may not know how to say what is true. But they have a sense of what is untrue, and can repudiate what they see to be incompatible with the faith which they have received.

This knowledge in the people Newman called the *consensus of the faithful*, the common mind of ordinary worshippers. Despite the feeling for structure, and hierarchy, and authority, he had a view of the nature of the Church in which the common man, the peasant, the housewife in the pew, mattered very much. This conviction sat uncomfortably among the middle-class respectabilities of Georgian England. It sat very uncomfortably amid the theories of the Church of Rome during those decades when it was at its most authoritarian. When Newman wrote (1859) a good article 'On Consulting the Faithful in Matters of Doctrine', a Roman Catholic bishop accused him of heresy, and cardinals in Rome were shocked. Newman discovered to his dismay that some bishops, and more priests, had a horror of the idea that laymen and laywomen had any other function in the Church save that of listening, obeying, and putting money into boxes.

To know the mind of the Church, teachers in the Church must look to the ordinary faith, ordinary practice, of ordinary Christian men. In many individual cases that will be wrong, or superstitious, or superficial. But these people are the Church, and deep in their corporate mind is a true intuition of what the Church is about. Therefore the teachers must 'consult' the lay Church, in two senses: passive, as one consults a barometer, to see how it behaves; and active, to take notice of its opinion. This is not the absurd idea that we must conduct polls into people's preferences. It is the conviction that within the body of Christian men and women is the experience of truth, and that this experience has something to say about new creeds or new ways of prayer. He defined this consensus of the Christian people as 'a sort of instinct'. He was sure of this: anyone who imagines the Church of Christ to be nothing but Popes, bishops, clergy, will have to rethink his divinity if he reads his history of the fourth century. 'There were untrustworthy councils, unfaithful bishops, there was weakness, fear of consequences, misguidance, delusion, hallucination, endless, hopeless, extending itself into nearly every corner of the Catholic Church.' He quoted a phrase of St Hilary of Poitiers: 'the ears of the common people are holier than the hearts of the priests' (C 77, 85).

And therefore, for all the necessary order of the Church, for all the pre-eminent place of its leaders, whose authority comes down from the apostles, each part of the Church has its proper function, and no part can be neglected. It is a great evangelical lesson, wrote Newman on this theme, that 'not the wise and powerful, but the obscure, the unlearned, and the weak constitute ... the real strength' of the Church (C 110).

'Securus judicat orbis terrarum'

Because Newman became a Roman Catholic he was sometimes accused of suffering a need, inside his psyche, for orders from on high, for a Pope's words to settle his doubts and hesitations. Newman's doubts and hesitations were sore. But in his change of allegiance he showed no signs of a desire to be the subject of ecclesiastical dictation. At one point in the process a famous saying of St Augustine pricked his mind: *Securus judicat orbis terrarum*; that is, if everyone agrees, the verdict must be right. Augustine used it against a small group in North Africa who contradicted the discipline of the international Church. It pricked Newman because suddenly he wondered about his national Church, the Church of England, in its differences from an international Church. The phrase *securus judicat* could be stretched to give a very authoritarian meaning – the international Church *is* the see of Rome, bow to its solitary edict. It could also be given a meaning which touched all the common people ('if everyone agrees ...'). This second meaning was present to Newman's mind. He did not become a Roman

Catholic because he wanted subjection to a Pope. He sensed that for him, and he believed for others, there would be a fuller share in that half-expressed mind of a common Christian people descending from the days of the first apostles until now.

The idea of development

Therefore, through the centuries, the Church *develops* its mind.

Any idea of development ran straight into the acute intellectual difficulty of that age: the nature of the changes in society or philosophy, which history proves.

Some Victorian Protestants taught that enquiry into the Bible showed that it was not all true. Was this new teaching wrong solely because it was new? And if it was not wrong, as those Protestants must say if they remained honest to truth, why are they still lawful heirs of the earliest Christians?

The early Church did not teach that bread and wine in the sacrament cease to be bread and wine. The modern Church of Rome taught that they do cease. It changed from the way in which the earliest Christians learnt about God. Was that wrong solely because it was change? And if it was not wrong, as Roman Catholics must say if they were to obey the Church, why are they still lawful heirs of the earliest Christians?

Conventional wisdom solved this difficulty by sleight of hand. It said that change was not change, it only looked like change. It made two suggestions:

1 New language is not the same as a new idea. We need new language to get an old idea right in new circumstances.

Someone said 'Jesus was a mere man.' The Church knew that this sentence was untrue to its conviction. It knew that though man he was not mere. So it framed new language to prevent anyone thinking that this was a Christian sentence. The conviction had not changed; only the words. New language guards old truth.

2 Logic is a good parallel. We know that $1 + 1 = 2$. Therefore we know that $400 + 400 = 800$. The truth is the same, but is different as a proposition. Is it true that Jesus smiled? He was man, and all men smile. It is logic.

How could Newman be satisfied with such explanations of the changes shown by history? He was educated a Protestant, and so taught to look for real change in the history of Catholicism. Then as an Oxford don he made a free study of the documents of early Christianity. He acquired that feeling for movement in history which a lot of men, Christian or non-Christian, acquired in those years.

He rejected neither new language, nor logic. He was satisfied by neither. They explained not enough of what had to be explained. The Church *moved* in history, and its movement was impossible to explain by the blind theory that it taught only the same doctrine in different words. And Newman never thought much of logic as a way of reaching truth.

Newman proposed a new use of the word *idea*. The Church has a deep inward secret consciousness of the truth. It sees a side of this and expresses what it sees. Later it sees another side, and expresses more. And therefore arising from the treasure-house which is the Christian consciousness of God the Church gradually expresses more and more of that consciousness.

The personal nature of the Essay on Development

The *Essay on the Development of Christian Doctrine* (1845) is strange, for very personal reasons.

Newman wrote at the height of his private debate whether, or when, or how, he should leave the Church of his childhood. He had persuaded himself that the Church of Rome was nearer in succession to the early Christian Church, and if he was so persuaded he must join. But he needed to work this out by historical example; both for his own mental happiness, and to give an account to enquirers.

This made the strangeness of the *Essay*. A problem for all the Churches of the nineteenth century was being tackled for the sake of a single mind's trouble about its own faith.

In essence the book is a sympathetic study of the early Church — its moods and principles and attitudes; its care about obedience to authority; the way it went about its business; its use of the Bible; its resistance to false teaching; its sacramental principles. Through and through, the *Essay* is a historical search for the axioms by which the early Church judged, and which would therefore flow in time into certain kinds of doctrine and reject other proposals for doctrine.

If a doctrine is taught now but was not taught by the earliest Christians, history must nevertheless be able to show how it was foreshadowed, *at least*, by hints and fragments of evidence. The records are scanty. Men's minds had not framed the words. Yet hints and fragments show that the Church's 'atmosphere' was *charged* with these ideas.

Newman took the case of reverence for relics. None of the doctrines about saints were taught by the earliest Christians. But the attitude towards the saints, and what the saints left behind, can be seen by history to be there from the first. The full flowering of monks and nuns was not there from the first. But history can show that the value set upon a holy single life was there from the first. The doctrines of the Virgin Mary were not full at the first. But history can show how the reverence for the Virgin which later issued in those doctrines was there from the first.

Interspersed in the pages of argument are rich and living portraits of the life of the early Christian Church. These are the best part of the book; and they are made the more interesting by the freshness of mind, and the new context, in which they are placed, with startling judgements thrown off in page after page; judgements always personal, usually original, sometimes brilliant, occasionally wild, very occasionally shocking – and giving the book its high interest for any student of the mind of the nineteenth century.

Yet the book does not persuade. It did not persuade Protestants, and in its detailed work, as distinct from its general proposal, it did not persuade Catholics. Part of this was basic, namely, the awkwardness of using historical evidence to prove any sort of case. Newman had this difficulty continuously before his own mind: the inadequacy of historical documents, the scraps of evidence, the silence where evidence is needed, the mass of evidence where evidence is useless, because men of the time did not bother to put down what they thought everyone knew, and put down in interminable homilies what no one could ever wish to know. A historian who saw the inadequacies of historical proof tried to use those inadequacies to make a historical proof — or rather, if not proof, sufficient of a historical guide to warrant himself in submitting to what his study made him believe the true successor of the Church of the apostles. He persuaded himself. He did not, by his argument as distinct from his proposal, persuade the reader.

When is a change a rightful development and when a corruption? Young birds do not grow into fish. But appearances are not all, because caterpillars do grow into butterflies. We need tests in Christian history, whether a change is right, that is, whether Catholicism is still Catholic, that is, whether the present Church is still faithful to the Church of the earliest Christians.

A large part of the book is devoted to providing seven tests for deciding whether a development is true or false, that is, whether it is the Church expressing its true mind or whether the novelty is a corruption. No one ever believed in the operation of these seven tests. No one believed in them when the book first came out and no one has believed in them since.

There was a second difficulty, that of a comparison. Newman was a historian. But he was a historian of the early Church. He knew little about the Reformation and less about the successors of the Reformation. Yet the purpose of his book was to contrast the early Church with 'modern Protestantism'. Reviewers saw how he made it easy for himself to cry *Protestantism is not historic Christianity* by defining Protestantism in terms which most Protestants repudiated.

The book had many passages of high interest as he meditated upon the nature of a philosophy of life as it passed through history; the ways in which it is received, and corrupted, and adapted, and made institutional. No one can understand Newman without studying the *Essay*. This was that unusual combination, a book unconvincing and yet seminal.

The question to be answered was narrow: How can a man who sees the life of the Roman Catholic Church as apostolic, but its doctrine as not wholly apostolic, reconcile these incompatibles and become a Roman Catholic with intellectual honesty?

But although the question was so personal and restricted and inward-looking, it touched on a great matter which Christendom had only lately begun to face. Everyone felt the movement of time, the changing nature of society. Everyone saw that all societies move in history, Churches just like States. Christendom, whether Protestant or Catholic, awoke to the crux of history; a gospel, given for all time, and then understood inside a ceaselessly changing environment with always new intellectual habits and always new moral predicaments. And Newman came along and honestly and openly recognised the impact of history upon the Churches.

The idea of development was the most important single idea which Newman contributed to the thought of the Christian Church. This was not because the idea of development did not exist already. But it was a very restricted idea, so restricted that it posed insuperable problems for anyone who studied history with open eyes. Newman made it wider and vaguer, and thereby far more fertile in conception, and more useful to anyone who cared about intellectual honesty, or the reconciliation of faith with the evidence of the past which history finds. Reviewers dismissed his arguments courteously or contemptuously. But in the long view the *Essay* was more weighty than one man's introspection of his predicament. That predicament happened to be only a single case to illustrate the predicament of Christendom.

5 Knowledge

Science and religion

In this philosophy of faith, it is obvious, science can never conflict with religion. The scientific findings of reason can never contradict the religious findings of conscience or vice versa. Science tells what is on this side of the barrier. Religion yearns for what is on the other side. Science and religion can never come to war. In its own sphere science is free, in its own sphere religion is free. When Darwin wrote about evolution, when newspapers wrote articles on the conflict between science and religion (the first such articles appeared in 1864), Newman was not moved. If assailants of Christianity say that the Church blocks the free advance of scientific enquiry, Newman can cheerfully deny any such charge. If science pretends to disprove God, Newman has every ground for telling it to mind its own business. Science pretends to nothing that is not this side of the veil, and here it is free, and every good Christian man must recognise its freedom. If the Church tries to deny the freedom of the scientist, so much the worse for the Church. It would pass outside the sphere of its action.

Of course this world is one, whether of matter or spirit. What is true this side of the veil cannot be untrue on the other. What is true on the other cannot be untrue on this side. All is God's world.

But – sometimes, the dictate of science *appears* to conflict with the dictate of religion. Newman so confessed. He took the instance of Christ's ascension into heaven (P 2.208).

The Bible, which our conscience is led to see as the vehicle of revealed truth, tells that Jesus ascended from earth into the sky. Physics says that the sky is neither up nor down. And where could he go? Do we say that the word 'ascended' is a mere popular expression because science dislikes? Newman will not dare to sit so lightly to the words of Scripture.

Therefore, apparent conflict. Then (says Newman) we must not try to judge between the two given 'truths'. We must remember our nothingness. We are shut in by the material world and cannot reach to things as they are. So we recognise that these two 'truths' are useful so far as they go — useful each in its own sphere, useful to act upon, useful as two separated approximations to a Truth which is greater than either.

Let us not hurry. 'When science crosses and breaks the received path of Revelation, it is reckoned a serious imputation upon the ethical character of religious men, whenever they show hesitation to shift at a minute's warning their position and to accept as truths shadowy views at variance with what they have ever been taught' (V 1.liii—liv). This takes no account of the difference between scientific discovery and religious truth. A scientist can throw off a startling theory and no one cares if he is wrong. If the Church adopts a theory which is later proved wrong, it matters, because its teaching affects the moral convictions of ordinary folk. The Church has responsibilities unknown to the individual who works away at his mathematics. To be slow in accepting what turns out in the end to be true, may be not dishonest but responsible. Therefore, no hurry.

Education

If you pack knowledge into a lot of young heads in schools, will adult society later be more virtuous?

Newman was scornful of this idea. Human nature is too giant to be chained by information. We have to overthrow passion. To suppose that we can do it by information is to behave like the ancient Lydians, who in a famine played at dice to try to forget their hunger.

The error lies in the belief that excellence comes from without. Excellence comes only from within. It cannot come if a child sits passive and receiving. It comes only through personal struggle and suffering. No one can be taught, no one can be interested, no one can be amused, into morality. Science or knowledge are powerless to heal the soul. Hearts need changing. Knowledge leaves us morally where we were before. It only makes us look and sound different. The notion that you can educate into virtue is pallid. It tinkers where it needs to recast.

In 1841 Sir Robert Peel made a speech opening a new reading-room near his home at Tamworth. The speech suggested that if people came there to read they would gain knowledge and be virtuous. Newman tore Peel's speech into shreds in a series of articles (*The Tamworth Reading Room*). It struck him as odd that by its rules only *virtuous* women might be admitted to read in that library. One would have expected the unvirtuous women to be the most glorious triumph of this theory of morality through knowledge.

Lurking under this controversy lay Newman's scepticism about the argument from the design of nature to a Designer. Peel thought that if his readers studied science, they would learn more about the world and therefore would know more about the creator of this world; that physics led towards belief in God. Newman said of Peel, 'he colours the phenomena of physics with the hues of his own mind'. 'To have recourse to physics to *make* men religious, is like recommending a canonry as a cure for the gout' (D 298–9).

The university

Since the beginning of the nineteenth century men had argued about the purpose of the university, and this was part of a bigger argument about the purpose of education. Is education designed to teach men to be able lawyers, or skilled engineers, or clergymen instructed in the language of the Bible, or sufficiently trained doctors of medicine? Is it meant to be useful in a man's life? If it is not meant to be useful why is it there? Can a future lawyer be as well instructed in a law school as in a university?

Newman loved the University of Oxford. In his time there that university was still part of the Church of England. Though his soul took flight from the Church of England, his heart stayed loyal to the place of learning where he learnt to think, and where he taught, and where he led a movement of religion.

Oxford had no difficulty in deciding on which side it stood in the long argument. It used the training of ancient language and literature as the instrument for training minds. Its opponents saw this attitude as provocative. When a boy has so few years to learn what he needs for his life, why should he be forced to spend long hours of precious time acquiring languages which he will never use, languages which they described as *dead*? But Oxford University did not doubt for a moment. And because Newman loved Oxford, and made intimate friendships at Oxford, and was taught to think for himself at Oxford, and lost neither the memory nor the gratitude, he could not doubt for a moment. Education is lowered if it is turned into the training of a man or a woman for a career.

This conviction became loud in Newman because he was made the head of a university. The Irish bishops invited Newman to be the first and founding head of a new university of Dublin. Newman accepted, on condition that he might remain superior of the Oratory at Birmingham.

The university opened in Dublin in November 1854 and Newman resigned office almost exactly four years later. His name and endeavours collected a good staff of lecturers. It did not work well. He was under the control of the Archbishop of Dublin, and the bishop liked to interfere where he did not understand. Newman was an Englishman; a convert; a mind with unconventional ideas; an Oxford don with notions that the university should be free; a teacher with the idea that under-graduates should think for themselves – all these were reasons why that Archbishop distrusted Newman. When Newman found that the Oratory suffered from his absences he took the occasion to resign, and the long work of building on the foundation was left to other hands.

Out of this venture in higher education came a noble book. It started as a course of lectures in 1852, before the university was open, entitled *Discourses on the Nature and Scope of University Education*. Then it turned with more matter into the book which we know as *The Idea of a University*. This book has remained the historic statement of an ideal of higher education which influenced Britain and through Britain the educational systems of many other countries.

Let us begin with some things which (in Newman's eyes) the university is not.

1 It is not a research institute. To research, undergraduates are a nuisance. Great research workers cannot be interrupted. They must hide themselves in caves or attics or laboratories or towers. The higher education of the young is part of the nature of the university. Naturally, any teacher worthy of the name is likely to advance the knowledge of his subject, and such advances in knowledge are part of the purpose of the university. But they arise out of its function as a place of education.

2 It is not a board of examiners, for certifying that young people have acquired a minimum of information. That can be done by post. 'A set of examiners with no opinions which they dare profess, and with no common principles, who are teaching or questioning a set of youths who do not know them, and do not know each other, on a large number of subjects, different in kind, and connected by no wide philosophy' — that is not a university (I 131). A university must be a community, or offer the chance of community — friendship between teacher and teacher, teacher and taught, and taught and taught. A young man has not only to learn information or ideas. He must see information or ideas in a context where others may see them in a different light; so that although education in a university starts by being an amassing of information, the university soon ceases to be only a place where young is taught by old, and becomes a place where the young start to contribute. In their little society undergraduates learn to think for themselves instead of swallowing passively. Knowledge of other persons, and the minds of others, and the way in which others think, and the light by which others see, is the essence of the university. 'A university is ... an Alma Mater, knowing her children one by one, not a foundry, or a mint, or a treadmill' (I 129).

3 A university is not content with the handing on of information. If it were content, it would not be a university. Its aim is the development of minds. Of course those minds need to gain a lot of information. No one can gain right judgement, which is part of a developed mind, if knowledge is sketchy. The

university must make it possible for its children to know much. It must make easy access to libraries or laboratories. But its aim is not the editing of human encyclopaedias. Knowledge is never to be measured by bulk. A load of information can weigh down the mind. You must be 'above' your knowledge, not sitting beneath its weight. It is the difference between a traveller in a flat plain, irritated because shut in by high hedges and green steeps and tangled wood, 'everything smiling indeed but in a maze'; and the same traveller climbing a hill or church tower to reconnoitre the lie of all that land. How many books have we all read which taught us everything and yet taught us nothing? 'We rise up, wondering at the learning which has passed before us, and wondering why it passed' (I 125).

4 If a university cannot be satisfied with cartfuls of knowledge, still less can it be satisfied with smatterings of knowledge. The world is full of men who are quick at repartee, and know a little about everything under the sun, and sound clever on platforms, and write brilliant articles in the newspapers, and are lively in conversation, and speak confidently to Houses of Parliament, but have no such education as the university can recognise. Though a university is a place where students may study everything in scholarship and science, it is not a place where students are to know about everything, for to know about everything is to know about nothing.

Still less is a university a place of 'accomplishments'. Newman's list of accomplishments that are not education amuses: drawing; fencing; general knowledge of plants or sea shells; stuffing birds; playing stringed instruments – these last two he called elegant pastimes or resources for the idle. He only gave these by way of illustration and the reader discerns the shadow of a far longer list hinted at by his intellectual severity.

The *enlargement* of mind which is the university's goal is not easily defined by Newman. We may say that the mind begins to understand how to use knowledge, how to judge it with criticism and yet with understanding, how to bring order into the information, how to perceive through the evidence something more important behind the evidence; how to move from the particular occasion towards general ideas. Not the equivalent of a reference book which a ready reader may pull down from his shelves to consult, it is part of the reader's constitution, a quality, an attitude. Not the passive receiving of knowledge, it is an active energetic force reducing knowledge to order as it is received; a digestion of new evidence into harmony with long acquired evidence; so that this trained faculty can rightly be called an illumination.

And Newman sang a hymn of praise to the vision:

> The intellect, which has been disciplined to the perfection of its powers, which knows ... which has learned to leaven the dense mass of facts and events with the elastic force of reason, such an intellect cannot be partial, cannot be exclusive, cannot be impetuous, cannot be at a loss, cannot but be patient, collected, and majestically calm ... It is the clear, calm, accurate vision and comprehension of all things, as far as the finite mind can embrace them ... It is almost prophetic from its knowledge of history; it is almost heart-searching from its knowledge of human nature; it has almost supernatural charity from its freedom from littleness and prejudice; it has almost the repose of faith, because nothing can startle it; it has almost the beauty and harmony of heavenly contemplation, so intimate is it with the eternal order of things and the music of the spheres. (I 123–4)

The five *almosts* in that hymn are weighty, as we shall see.

Here then, cast into Utopian language, is the ideal of a university; the trained mind, formed on the study of one or more arduous disciplines, which it has shared with other students and with its teachers, so that it knows how to judge every variety of new knowledge and through that to move towards a true apprehension of all the world and of man.

This is not useful? On the contrary, nothing could be more useful. The traveller along the road towards such an ideal of knowledge cannot but perceive much that is fresh in the landscape on either side of that road. What is necessary is to pursue the goal for its own sake, and not because it is useful. Turn education into professional training and it is corrupt. Pursue knowledge for its own sake, and at last it will transform the possibilities in professional training.

> Nothing is excellent, beautiful, perfect . . . for its own sake, but it overflows, and spreads the likeness of itself all around . . . If the intellect is so excellent a portion of us, and its cultivation so excellent, it is not only beautiful, perfect, admirable and noble in itself, but in a true and high sense it must be useful to the possessor and to all around him; not useful in any low, mechanical, mercantile sense, but as diffusing good, or as a blessing, or a gift, or power, or a treasure, first to the owner, then through him to the world. (I 144)

Even in the last decades of the twentieth century we could do worse than vote an Act of Parliament that every Minister of Education, or vice-chancellor, shall pass an examination in Newman before he takes office.

Now comes the question of religion in the university. This was central to Newman's point in three ways:

1 The quest for knowledge depends on moral states like humility of mind or freedom from drunkenness or lust. Yet over these moral states the intellect has no hold.

'Quarry the granite rock with razors, or moor the vessel with a thread of silk; then may you hope with such keen and delicate instruments as human knowledge and human reason to contend against those giants, the passion and the pride of man' (I 111). Mind cannot be separated from soul. And the soul needs God to be free. Education alone is not enough.

The book is very extraordinary in its contrast between the intellect's success and faith; the glory and yet the everlasting insufficiency of mind. It is contrast, not tension. There is no sense of tension. This is one of the elements in the *Idea* which make it unique. No one ever sang a lovelier song in praise of education for its own sake. And in the same moment no one ever denied so eloquently its natural crown.

2 Newman thought that an institution which failed to provide for the study of religion was not a university. Why? Because a

university is there to study the great experiences of mankind; and no one can deny that religion is weighty in the experience of mankind. A university which abolished all study of the physical and biological sciences, or all study of anthropology, would not be a university. So with provision for the study of religion.

3 Newman believed that the Church must control religious teaching in a university. At Oxford he argued that the Church of England, at Dublin he argued that the Church of Rome, must control. This does not mean that the Church should try to stop scientists reaching whatever conclusions they think true. Nor does it mean that censors should bowdlerise great literature to make it moral and good for young minds. The university is 'not a convent . . . not a seminary; it is a place to fit men of the world for the world' (I 197). What was important to Newman was the presence of the truth about God leavening the minds of the different faculties.

For writing this classic book he consulted the other recent Catholic university at Louvain; and he had a nodding acquaintance with what happened in Scotland. But Oxford was the fountain of this book; not Oxford as it was or is, but Oxford as it might be if visions ever came true. Here is a book upon the design of a Catholic university, derived in main part from an idealised vision of a university which then formed part of the Church of England. The date of 9 October 1845, when he changed his religious denomination, was far less important to the understanding of his ideas than he himself, and his later interpreters, supposed.

6　The image of the Church of Rome

In the first half of his life he wound up the Church of England to its Catholic heritage. In the second half of his life he wound down the Church of Rome – that is, he sought to persuade its leaders not to push their Catholicity into fanaticism, or superstition, or irrationality, or rigid hierarchy; and therefore to keep their minds open to the old principle of primitive Catholic faith, and from that broader base to listen to the discoveries of the age – the advance of historical method, before his death the progress of criticism of the Bible; but above all to remember that Catholicism is a mystery of the spirit, too glorious and too profound for the tidiest minds to limit; and that faith in God is always more real and more certain than the language which seeks to describe faith in God.

To persuade the Church to keep its mind open was very delicate work. It could only be done by someone seen to be loyal to traditional Catholicism. Yet in those years of the 1860s and '70s when Italian nationalists treated the Pope outrageously, anyone who suggested an open mind was thought to be a liberal, and a liberal was thought to be a compromiser, and a compromiser was a rat. Therefore the work required exceptional finesse.

Newman felt a religious duty of respect for rightful superiors. This sense of obligation mingled with a free mind to produce curious consequences. One critic said of Newman's mind that it was a magnificent intelligence which seemed to cherish a passion for bondage. This is not the Newman who comes out of the private letters. He loathed the constrictions on his freedom of thought. He wore the chains with an excess of hatred. They gripped him less tightly than sometimes he fancied.

He came to regard the work of the theologian as like dancing on a tightrope some hundred feet above the ground – surely the strangest idea of theology ever to be penned by a famous divine, and only to be explained by his unique combination of principles, neither to lose his freedom of mind nor to be thought a heretic by authority. Any other thinker with Newman's independence would have damned authority and said that truth is truth whatever illiterate critics might say in their bureaux. Newman had too deep a sense of the authority and responsibility of the teaching Church.

His method was as follows: he answered Protestant critics. In answering he told the critics that they misunderstood what Catholicism was about, and that its mind was far more open than in their prejudice they believed. This helped Protestants to be gentler and dispelled prejudice. More important, it represented Catholicism to Catholics as a community of honest and thinking persons.

Newman owed this chance to members of the Church of England who attacked the Church of Rome. He was very fortunate that among the attackers were four very famous Anglicans, perhaps the four most famous Anglicans. In chronological order of his replies they were (1) Charles Kingsley, celebrated as a novelist, and the Regius Professor of Modern History at Cambridge; (2) Dr Pusey, Regius Professor of Hebrew at Oxford, and the leader of what was left of the Oxford Movement since Newman abandoned the cause; (3) Mr Gladstone, once Newman's disciple, and at the moment of attack a former Prime Minister; and (4) Newman's earlier self, in his own ferocious onslaughts on the Church of Rome.

Kingsley

When Newman had been a Roman Catholic for fifteen and a half years, he was libelled. Kingsley accused him of saying that truth need not, and on the whole ought not, to be a virtue with the Roman Catholic clergy. When asked by Newman where he was alleged to have said this, Kingsley referred to a sermon preached twenty years before – that is, *while Newman was still a clergyman of the Church of England*.

Thus the charge mounted monstrously; from being a passing libel into an accusation that he was a hypocrite and knave while he was a clergyman in the Church of England. Kingsley put Newman's whole career under scrutiny. Newman (alleged Kingsley) reached Roman Catholic convictions long before he publicly professed Roman Catholic faith. Therefore Kingsley challenged him to tell the world what was the meaning of 9 October 1845. What was the inwardness of mind and heart at that moment? What states of mind prepared for the last leap? Was he really a secret Catholic before 1845, and if he was, was he conscious of it or unconscious? And these personal questions could only be answered if he described more than his private opinions. He started with a simple faith of a child and grew to profess the intellectual faith of an Oxford don – what was the growth from one to the other? He grew to have an understanding of what was meant by the word Catholic – in this growth had he learnt from the English tradition of divinity? In short, is a Protestant always more than half a Catholic? Is a Protestant always a 'secret Catholic' (if he is a true Christian man) because he understands truth in a way which has much in common with a Catholic understanding of truth? And is a Catholic always more than half a Protestant?

Newman's chance was wonderful. Under his pressure Kingsley withdrew. But the withdrawal was grudging and blustered. It was fortunate that by 1864 Newman was not a saint. If he had been nearer heaven he would have accepted Kingsley's apology and not whipped a man on the ground. But this was not only a Catholic priest defending the honour of all priests. Once he had been the liveliest controversialist among the dons of Oxford University. He needed to explain himself to himself; to try to understand what happened, and how it happened, at Littlemore on 9 October 1845. And he had the occasion to set the image of the Church of Rome in a light new to British history since the Reformation.

The Apologia pro vita sua

The result was the *Apologia pro vita sua*.

Men marvelled that Newman could have written the *Apologia* during only three months of 1864. They talked of an almost miraculous power of concentration. But this is very easy to explain. Without intending to write this book, he prepared to write it for three or four years. He meditated on his earlier career, sorted letters, arranged, copied, annotated, collected. When his entire life was challenged, he hardly needed to think what to say. Almost all the material lay at his fingertips. He checked a few dates and facts with old friends, but the substance he only had to write down. A man who imagined that he had more enemies than he had, but who had enemies, and who knew himself to need defending, and who believed that a defence was possible, was suddenly confronted with an invitation, if not a necessity, to pen that defence. The challenge forced an auto-biographer *manqué* into his self-justification.

He was accused of being a deceiver, since 1841 or earlier. He had been no loyal member, it was said, of the Church of England. He had played with its words, and twisted them for his purposes, and was really a Roman Catholic while he pretended to be a Protestant. He was perfidious.

Therefore he could not answer solely with a history of his opinions. The opinions had to be part of a living man, personal, seen in his private and public context, full of memory and affection and anxiety. This made the *Apologia* readable. He was not dealing in arguments of thirty years before, as faded as the dead speeches in old Hansards. He dealt in states of mind, fluid, elusive, personal, merging insensibly, a man intelligible because alive.

He felt, and could probe his own feelings delicately, even into the shadows of psychological speculation. He had a trained sense of historical development. Above all, he had that sense of continuity which could look at the past with a straight eye and a generous heart.

This is the book by which the world came to know Newman. Drawn from letters and wholly sincere, it nevertheless misled by its selection. It omitted much of the man. It gave the impression that he always lived in another world, and it knew nothing of his music, interests, general reading, acts as leader of a party. The reader would not know that this was a famous preacher. It was modest, and attributed to others what should be attributed to himself.

He tried to describe how a young man who cared about truth first found it in a Church and then realised that he had only found a part and that the fullness of truth lay elsewhere; and how he went elsewhere, and was now assured that he had found what he sought.

For the first time in all literature a convert described the history of his conversion with hardly a note of convertitis. Like any other convert he had passed through the fire of strong emotion. Yet he could recount what happened with calmness, with a fair and accurate portrait of his earlier sympathies, and the reality of his nobler aspirations when he was a Protestant. For the first time in English history, a Roman Catholic priest rejoiced publicly in many of the truths taught by Protestants.

The answer to Pusey

Seeing that the ice wall between Canterbury and Rome had a chance of being melted by Newman's *Apologia*, Dr Pusey wrote a plea for peace between the Churches, called the *Eirenicon*. But living remote in a corner of Christ Church at Oxford and never quite able to judge the effect of his words, Pusey spent most of the time telling the world what were the main obstacles to unity, which were the errors of the Church of Rome, and therefore his olive branch looked, as Newman said, as though it were discharged from a catapult.

This was the second chance which Newman needed. He answered Pusey without compromise (*Letter to Dr Pusey on the Occasion of his Eirenicon* (1866)).

The answer to Gladstone

Gladstone wrote a pamphlet against the Pope called *The Vatican Decrees in their Bearing on Civil Allegiance*. Among other harsh words he said that anyone who accepted the Pope's infallibility would not be likely to be a loyal citizen of Great Britain. Many people then wrote pamphlets against Gladstone. The only reply that mattered was Newman's reply, published early in 1875. It was entitled *A Letter to the Duke of Norfolk on Occasion of Mr Gladstone's Recent Expostulation*. It was the last of Newman's controversial pamphlets.

The controversialist had grown in moral stature. As an Anglican he slaughtered the Roman Catholic Church with scorn and satire, and with the other barrel of his gun made the Lady Margaret Professor look more ridiculous than he was and the Regius Professor of Divinity more heretical than his books warranted. As a new Roman Catholic he slaughtered the Church of England with scorn and satire; he whipped Achilli, and trampled upon one of the famous writers of England in his answer to Kingsley. But now the old pamphleteer was to his opponents the charmer that he always was to his friends, and the whipping phrases disappeared from what he wrote.

He acquired a new virtue, forbearance. Two years later he publicly shed his younger controversialist self by applying to himself a condemnation of language fitting in a parliament or public meeting or court of law but unfitting in an ecclesiastic (V 1.xxviii). An unregenerate reader may regret the growth in grace.

The answer to himself

Two years after the answer to Gladstone he published a reply to his own earlier self.

As vicar of St Mary's in Oxford he was in the habit of giving lectures in a side-chapel. One of these courses was published in 1837 as *Lectures on the Prophetical Office of the Church*. Parts of the lectures were fierce against Low-Church Protestants. Parts were very fierce against Roman Catholics.

From 1868 to 1881 he republished most of his Anglican works. That a priest should publish works of divinity from a period which he now repudiated was unusual enough to cause muttering. At first it happened naturally. After the *Apologia* he was again famous instead of notorious. People asked bookshops for his works; especially the sermons from the pulpit of St Mary's. But because this was unusual, he did not republish them himself. He planned it; but the volumes were edited by a

Protestant, once Newman's curate, Copeland, who insured Newman against trouble by a little confession at the beginning that there would be sentences which Dr Newman would now wish altered or omitted. Later on Copeland made a selection of the volumes into one volume, and had the aim to make Roman Catholics and Anglicans understand each other's devotion better.

Once the Roman Catholic world was accustomed to a Roman theologian publishing Anglican works of theology, the muttering diminished; and Newman now started to republish systematically without any need for an editor. The texts needed scissors if not paste, and certainly notes, if they were to be acceptable in his new world; and this process makes the editing of Newman's works a headache for modern commentators. Often he made subtle alterations and no one can see why.

In 1877 he republished the *Lectures on the Prophetical Office*. They were printed as part of a collection with a different title, *The Via Media*, with new notes and a long preface. This long preface was intended to demolish the theory of the Church which he taught in the Church of England and which many of his successors there still professed. He treated himself coldly — as an enemy like Kingsley — and referred to himself in a distant third person.

The image

In these four answers, to Kingsley, Pusey, Gladstone and himself, he did what he could to clear away Protestant prejudice and remind Catholics that narrowness fitted Catholicism ill.

Punch always caricatured Newman as sinister, sly, underhand. This was a widespread though hazy impression of Roman Catholic priests. Newman took the picture to pieces. Men who died for their faith in an epidemic of cholera were men of honour and openness and directness. And the *Apologia* was written with a very conscious sincerity, by an author aware that enemies would pounce upon the least hint of special pleading. No reader can miss the attempt at total honesty. The *Apologia* altered the subsconscious portrait of a Roman Catholic priest in the minds of many educated Britons.

The second element of the average Englishman's portrait came from travel in Europe. Tourists went into a church in Naples and found an old crone superstitious and credulous before a crucifix or a statue. *This* was Roman Catholic faith, a compound of superstition and credulity, a substitution of Mary and the saints for the pure worship of the one God.

But the woman in the gospel who touched the hem of Jesus's garment to be healed, she was credulous and superstitious. Christ tolerated her superstition because he saw it as a sign of a simple faith. The Church would like to be rid of superstition. But its bishops do not wish to root out faith in weeding up credulity. Sometimes we have to be silent before excess. If a people is convinced that a picture or crucifix works miracles, he is a crude irreverent pastor who destroys the picture or crucifix, for he needs to think of the simple faith and to bide his time. If the Church treated popular superstition so roughly, it would endanger 'the faith and loyalty of a city or district, for the sake of an intellectual precision which was quite out of place'. If the bishop knows the cult to be false, he must try to quell. But 'errors of fact may do no harm, and their removal may do much'. 'We may surely concede a little superstition, as not the worst of evils, if it be the price of making sure of faith' (V 1.lxv—lxix).

This argument was the more impressive from one who patently felt in himself the solitariness of the soul, alone before its Maker. 'The Catholic Church allows no image of any sort ... no saint, not even the Blessed Virgin herself, to come between the soul and its Creator. It is face to face' (A 177).

Devotional language is likely to run to excess. If you love someone you use terms of endearment in private which if printed in a newspaper look maudlin, repulsive as love-letters in a police report (Diff 80). The early Church glorified the Virgin far more than Protestants like to remember. But Newman threw overboard an excess of adulation of St Mary, 'fulsome frigid flattery'. These things, he said, may suit foreigners, that is their affair. They do not suit Englishmen and they do not suit me.

The third component of British hostility rested on the idea of an infallible authority. Must not an intelligent man, who submitted his belief to whatever a Pope ordered, enter 'a degrading bondage' (A 221)?

This was Newman's chief difficulty in lightening the image of his Church.

Even as an Anglican he believed that the Catholic Church could not err. When he changed his Church he had no difficulty about fitting the authority of the Pope into his belief. We need strong authority in religion, to resist the aggressive intellect of man, interfering where it has no right.

He did not want the bishops to define the Pope as infallible. He thought that the Church needed to do a lot more thinking before it cleared its own mind on what precisely it meant. History showed that Popes had erred. Newman was sure that the Pope was not infallible if he opened his mouth in casual conversation. To stop the bishops defining, Newman did what he could. It was exceedingly little. When at the Vatican Council of 1870 they insisted on defining that the Pope is infallible whenever he makes formal decisions on faith and morals, and even though the Church at large has not formally expressed its agreement, he cheerfully accepted what was decided though he was still not sure what was meant. He was quite serene. The Church will meditate further, and one day will give further light.

Meanwhile Protestants were more than contemptuous at what was done. The more extreme felt glee that, by so defining, the Church of Rome should destroy its credibility among thinking men.

Newman therefore expounded the limits of the infallible authority.

1 It touches only religion. It cannot touch science. The physicists and the Darwinians are still free. Its sphere is religious truth; not an inch further.

2 Its sphere is only what has already been given by the

apostles to the Church. It cannot make us believe new truth. It can only safeguard old truth. 'Nothing can be presented to me, in time to come, as part of the faith, but what I ought already to have received, and hitherto have been kept from receiving (if so) merely because it has not been brought home to me' (A 227).

3 The object of the authority can never supersede the dictate of the individual conscience. Newman wrote one of those sentences most offensive to cardinals in Rome.

'If I am obliged to bring religion into after-dinner toasts (which indeed does not seem quite the thing) I shall drink, − to the Pope if you please − still to Conscience first, and to the Pope afterwards' (Diff 261). If authority interferes in secular matters of philosophy or science or literature or history, it may demand silence. It claims to censure books and authors. It cannot demand internal submission, only external silence. This, said Newman, is the great trial to reason presented by the authority of the Church (A 230).

In strong language he denounced Roman Catholic extremists. These extremists treated every moderate as disloyal to the Pope. They regarded *minimisers* with loathing. In that moment of papal history maximisers dominated the Church. Newman was courageous. He identified himself with the minimisers.

> What I feel deeply, and ever shall feel, while life lasts, is the violence and cruelty of journals and other publications, which, taking as they professed to do the Catholic side, employed themselves by their rash language (though, of course, they did not mean it so), in unsettling the weak in faith, throwing back inquirers, and shocking the Protestant mind. Nor do I speak of publications only; a feeling was too prevalent in many places that no one could be true to God and His Church, who had any pity on troubled souls, or any scruple of 'scandalizing those little ones who believe in' Christ.

Minimising is the true duty because it does not multiply doctrines to be believed without necessity. He wrote an intentionally comic sentence; men may *maximise* if they like as long as they do not *dogmatise* (Diff 2.300, 365).

In all the later part of his life Newman did what he could for the Catholic Church. In both parts of his life he had a common principle, unwavering: the quest for the Catholic heritage. During the later years he ran greater risks, because the Curia had more bite than the gentle old Anglican Bishop of Oxford. He must lessen prejudice. He must weaken extremism. And he must do all this in total loyalty to his Church or he would not be heard. The cardinals in Rome kept wondering whether he should be made to recant some of his bolder sentences.

The professional theologians, whose minds were as closed as oysters, were unhappy to be told, by his idea of development, that the Church must respect the findings of historians; or that common people sometimes had a deeper idea of faith than clergymen, or even Popes; or that devotional practices ought to be quiet and restrained. The most unpleasing of Roman *Monsignori* wrote to the Archbishop of Westminster, that 'Dr Newman is the most dangerous man in England.'

The cardinal

In 1878 a new Pope was elected as Leo XIII. Next year, to everyone's surprise, he offered Newman a cardinal's hat. Newman nearly refused and then accepted.

Long ago he denounced as depraved appetite the desire to be praised by a multitude whom we have never seen; deeply criminal, he said, an odious superfluous wanton sin (P 8.178). He found it more agreeable to the Christian temper to know and be known by a few and to grow in their esteem and affection. He used to think about men and women old and ill, living on though they seemed to serve no good purpose, and at death unnoticed by their fellows; and he thought of these as the type of true Christians, unknown even to friends and still serving their Master. *Eminence*, he once said, made much intercourse with the world into a duty, and so tended to draw the mind from God (P 7.62).

If he had stuck to his refusal it would have been more fitting to the man. The glory of Newman is the contempt he had for parade; the feeling that he was not somebody and ought not to look like somebody; the absence of pretentiousness — quiet, restrained, peaceable in his cell, not a man for splashes in the world. The personality would have been more rounded if he had stuck to his refusal, and gone down to the grave as old Father Newman, in his dingy black cassock, the rather disreputable priest whom authority could not think quite loyal, the failure from a distant past. The grandeur of Newman lay not in a red hat but in decades of suffering by reason of his mental constitution. Some archbishops needed to be cardinals to win stature. For Newman the office could have no such consequence. The old Roman Cato said that he preferred people to ask why there was no statue to his memory than why there was a statue.

The ends of man are not designed to make a soul seem of pure consistency. A refusal would not have served his Church, nor Catholicism, nor Christianity. He stood for attitudes which needed to break through the ring of party line if the Catholics of the twentieth century were not to retreat into a ghetto. The cardinal's hat fitted the man ill, and was necessary to the future of his causes.

Perhaps he saw this dimly. His main motive was the old one, obedience to the Church. And then he could discern how the semi-rebel, up against cardinals and bishops, papal chamberlains and illiterate censors, had come through at last and triumphed. In accepting the hat he lost nothing of his unpomp. The cassock remained as dingy, and the mental attitude did not alter.

No act ever proved so resoundingly the importance of a mere title. From every practical point of view the office made no difference to Newman, except to force an old man into a dreary journey to Rome to receive the hat. He had no more influence on Roman policy than before. He was still a withdrawn old man saying his prayers at an Oratory in Birmingham. People appealed to him to use his influence to get things done, and he knew, though they could not, that his influence to such ends was still nothing.

But from the point of view of the future — of the development of Catholic thought — of the freedom of Catholic minds and

their concern for truth — the act was of immeasurable importance. This was recognition by a Pope. To make a man a cardinal
was not to approve all his ideas or clear all his utterances of
heresy. But it acclaimed the general work; and that work
included friendliness to Protestants, assent to the place of
history in the development of Christian thought, recognition of
the free rights of critical enquiry, recognition that scientists are
free to follow their arguments wherever they lead, antipathy to
extremist forms of doctrine or devotion, confession that the
great secret body of lay Christians was also the Church and not
slaves of a hierarchy. If Newman had not become Cardinal
Newman, posterity could more easily have disregarded his work.
When he accepted his cardinal's hat he made a speech saying
that his life's work had tried to counter liberalism. But, really,
he stood for vital intellectual principles and their rightful place
in a Catholic Church. No Catholic thinker exercised more
influence on the thought of the twentieth century.

When Newman left the Church of England, Dr Pusey con-
soled himself for the calamity by saying that perhaps Providence
intended him to do much good to the Church of Rome. This did
not happen in ways which Pusey expected. But the prophecy
came true.

7 A fight against liberalism?

In the Rome of 1879 to say that Newman stood for the fight against liberalism caught popularity, for at that moment of history the word stood for the vices of the Italian government as it maltreated the Pope. But Newman did not use such a word to gain applause. He believed this about himself. And he was under a delusion about himself. And this delusion is important to the right understanding of Newman's mind.

Liberalism is a vague word.

Newman was fourteen years old when the Battle of Waterloo was fought. He grew to manhood as Europe turned against the French Revolution. Newman's Oxford Movement was part of that European swing towards tradition in religion which was the devout accompaniment of political conservatism and was found in Protestant countries equally with Catholic.

In the epoch of the Reform Bill, from 1831 onwards, the young don was a stout Tory. He called the Whigs vermin. He thought it monstrous that a Whig government should try to steal the money of the Church for secular ends, or abolish bishoprics without asking the Church, or force Oxford University to accept dissenters among its undergraduates. He believed that clergymen should not be members of a political party. But they should do all they could for the better side in politics. He gained the reputation of being a young bigot.

He mellowed.

His philosophy of life was conservative even though he sometimes disapproved of the Conservative Party. Its centre was continuity and development. That is, expect change because change cannot but happen to society, but see that the change grows out of and conserves the best of the past. This was not compatible with die-hard Toryism. It was the thought of Edmund Burke, and thereafter of all sane and moderate conservatives.

His doctrine of a corrupt humanity aligned him with

conservatives. Whatever the constitutional arrangements we make, society will be in part unjust, and its machinery imperfect because that is what man is like. Even if all the members of the society were Christians, the society would still be in part unjust. Newman could not abide the doctrine of inevitable advance in human society. He was violent against the idea of progress.

He also thought that religion is the bond of society, which depends not upon policemen but upon consent. You cannot make men behave by law, at least not for long. You cannot make them virtuous by education. A healthy society cannot do without religion. And this has a faintly conservative undertone, because it pushes religion towards the side of law and order.

All this made him a moderate conservative in political theory. But he was to the left of such a theory in its practical working. This was due to his status as a dissenter after he became a Roman Catholic.

He held that Queen Victoria could do nothing of her own will, and dared to compare her to one of the do-nothing kings of early France. He held that Churches contribute to the freedom of society, and by their nature help to defend the common people from the power of the State. He had no use for government by committees, which he thought would cover England with monstrosities in architecture and make the country into a paradise for little men. He wanted the State to interfere as little as possible with individual freedom, except in time of war. He recognised that the weakness of a liberal State caused ill, but believed that in Britain this was made good by the vigour and individuality of the people, a nation of private enterprise, best left by government without meddling. The State rests on consent.

In the Victorian age this was not an illiberal standpoint. He was far to the left of the Roman Catholics who obeyed the moods of contemporary Rome. He believed in the rightness of the secular State, neutral between denominations, although the then Pope condemned the idea. He believed in toleration of all faiths, although the then Pope condemned that idea. He regarded absolute government as intolerable, although the then Pope was not unfriendly to that system of polity.

Evidently, when he professed himself to have spent his life fighting liberalism, it was not political liberalism that he fought, except in the hectic years 1829–33.

But liberalism had a religious meaning. On this subject Newman made various not quite compatible statements. If we boil them down, they come to this:

Liberalism sometimes means intellectual brashness, and all such brashness is the way not to find the truth. Liberalism sometimes means that dogmas are not to be accepted. But the Church must frame its experience in dogmas. Only so can the experience be handed from one generation to another. Liberalism sometimes means that all religious faith is to be tested by (secular) reason. But on Newman's theory such reason cannot reach beyond the veil and so is incapable of testing religious truth.

Darwin wrote *The Origin of Species*, and Colenso, Bishop of Natal, proved with absurd arithmetic that the history of the earlier Old Testament is unreliable, and all Europe was in ferment over the 'conflict between science and religion'. Everyone with open eyes could see the intellectual trouble among the educated, the growth of doubt, the widening of the area where the devout say that they do not know. What of *dogma* in this new world where all the Churches are found to be teaching as true what was shown to be untrue? Could the religion of society, so inseparable from the morals of society, depend upon believing that a real woman tempted a real man with an apple?

In their perplexity or anxiety religious minds appealed to the leading thinkers of England to help them, and to show how the creed still stood despite Darwin and despite Colenso. As Newman was a Christian leader, he received such appeals for help, from Protestants as well as Catholics. Would he not 'champion' revealed truth?

Newman knew that he stood for Christian truth. But, he asked himself, what was it that he was against? Certainly he was not against science, nor against scientists making their enquiries and their discoveries; that is, unless they misused their position to go outside their province and say, for example, that they proved that there is no God. When he examined his mind, he asked himself whether he was against 'honest-doubters'; that is, sincere and religious minds perplexed by the new discoveries or theories; and he knew that for them he felt nothing but compassion, and said that the only people who should be fierce with them were people who had no experience of the difficulty of discerning truth amid error. No one yet knew whither these scientific theories were to lead the human mind, and only a rash man would stand forth now as 'the champion of revealed truth' when he could not yet identify the foe. What are we then to do? 'Be patient . . . have a little faith and fortitude' (A 235). He was sure that, though the teaching authority of the Church is infallible, it could never make decrees on physical subjects, because on physical subjects it had no power to decree.

The fact is, what Newman denounced as liberalism, no one else regarded as liberalism. And this led to misunderstanding. Men supposed that Newman was illiberal because he kept saying so, and because he refused to recant when he was pressed. People supposed that the young bigot of 1834 must be the essential Newman. But no one who reads his later works, or ponders his private letters, can possibly think this to be true.

When he came back from Rome after receiving his Cardinal's hat and making his last speech against 'liberalism', he expected never to write again. But he found that for the Church, in its quandary over liberalism, he could still do something.

At the core of European 'apostasy' was the Bible. Genesis was not (all) true history. The Churches said that it was (all) true history. You could not trust the Churches any longer.

In the 1860s, when first the argument over science versus religion was fierce, Newman suffered the illusion of other Roman Catholics that Protestants were in a mess and the Church of Rome was not. For Protestants made the Church rest upon the Bible whereas Rome made the Bible rest upon the Church. But as the argument developed, and new knowledge was sifted, and the problem was pondered, Newman came to see – he was one of the first Catholics to see – that this new knowledge was just as awkward for the Church of Rome as for the Protestants; in one respect more awkward, for the Church of Rome, with its claims to certainty of faith, and its use of words like *infallibility*, found it hard to face, with anything but denial, the assertion, 'you can trust the Churches no longer'. Yet mere denial was useless. New knowledge had been won. In the long run a Church which failed to face the facts condemned itself to occupy an intellectual ghetto in the world.

The subject was dangerous. Newman felt an obligation to try. At the age of eighty-two he published in *The Nineteenth Century* (February 1884) an article on the inspiration of Scripture. When this was assailed by an Irish professor of theology, he printed a second article, called 'Postscript'.

The modern reader of Newman on the inspiration of the Bible feels that he reads what is obsolete: an old man tackling a non-problem with out-of-date principles. This feeling is a failure in historical understanding. The mind of the then Church of Rome was shut. It could listen to no proposal that any fragment of the Bible was not true. Somehow that mind had to be prised ajar. And if the reader feels that Newman prised it only a chink, when he ought to have pushed harder to let in fresh air, that is also a failure in historical understanding. Churches will not readily accept anything which, as they fear, will weaken their influence over the morals of a people. If Newman shocked Catholics, he could only hurt. He must prise open the door in such a way as to help intelligent Catholics while they saw that his mind was still Catholic. In this delicate work the cardinal's hat, and the prestige, were not disadvantages.

By the standards of that day he allowed very much. The Bible is not necessarily true as science or history, only in what it says on faith and morals – though some statements of history may be intimately connected with faith. We need not believe that Old Testament prophets knew of their New Testament fulfilments; or that Isaiah is a book by a single author; or that the Gospel texts always agree because the witnesses cannot err. And we are not bound to believe what is said 'in passing' but has nothing to do with faith or morals. St Paul says he left a cloak at Troas.

It is no part of Christian doctrine to suppose that St Paul might not be mistaken about the place where he forgot his cloak.

This argument by Newman is now so obvious that it is hardly worth pursuing. But in the year 1884 it was not conservative. It disturbed other Catholics besides the Irish professor of divinity. It was acceptable to very few. And it came as a blessed relief to the handful of Catholic scholars whose minds accepted the advances of history, and who saw the mental cul-de-sac into which authority seemed to propel the Church.

Newman made two provisos. Both were characteristic. We owe a first duty to simple people. If they will be disturbed by what we think about history in the Bible then it is better to keep silent. 'The household of God has claims upon our tenderness in such matters which criticism and history have not' (T 105). Secondly, we owe respect to what has been generally received, even if no authority in the Church has laid down what must be received.

8 The acceptance of Newman

When Newman left the Church of England, he thought himself repudiated by that Church. He had tried to wind up his Church, which refused, he imagined, to be wound. In truth, if he could have known it, he had won. The Church of England would look back upon the days of Newman's Oxford Movement as days to which its spirituality owed a permanent debt.

For the Church of England the loss was disaster. Until his last unsettlement, this mind was in the authentic tradition of its spirituality and doctrine. He was on the way to being another Lancelot Andrewes. The Church of England was to possess eminent philosophers and historians during the nineteenth century but few enough systematic thinkers on doctrine and only one other with such a command of the English language. They resented his departure, and tried to forget him.

Forty years later their feelings had changed. It was curious. Most of the English still feared the Pope. They still associated his religion with the burning of Latimer, the Spanish Armada, a conspiracy to blow up the House of Commons, or Jacobite rebellion. During the Victorian age their antipathy grew sharper instead of less tolerant, as the wave of Irish immigrants threatened the jobs of British working men and helped to hold down their wages. Their opinion had not changed. Yet they rejoiced to see Newman a cardinal. Something in him now felt very English; certainly not Italian, perhaps not even quite popish in the full sense; and a man whose words were beloved on many non-Catholic lips.

Early in life, becalmed in the strait between Sardinia and Corsica, he wrote stanzas which perfectly represented his later and mature ideal of life; the man of quiet, troubled in mind often, searching for the mystery of God and usually baffled in the pursuit, surrounded by clouds; but moving slowly in faith, content to see a little at a time, making no distant plan nor long calculation; doing the day's work, one thing ahead at a time, and looking upward when he could. The first stanza ran:

> Lead, kindly light, amid the encircling gloom,
>   Lead thou me on!
> The night is dark, and I am far from home —
>   Lead thou me on!
> Keep thou my feet; I do not ask to see
> The distant scene — one step enough for me.

The Victorian generation found itself in this language. Unsure about the Bible, afraid of Marx and class-war, agonised by evolution and the hostility of nature, hesitant over its moral foundations, struggling with slums and exploitation — later Victorians heard Newman's stanzas, made them their own, and voiced their own hesitant act of faith. Whether or not he was the Pope's man, he was theirs.

When Newman became a cardinal he thought that he was near his grave. But he lived another eleven years at the Oratory. He spent his time in quiet, and the meditative prayer, which is half memory, of the very old; and read with interest, and not without criticism, books about the Oxford Movement; and suffered from pangs of regret about the time that he lost through so many years. He died on 11 August 1890, and was buried in the Oratory grave at Rednal near Birmingham, his body with the body of Ambrose St John. On the pall at his funeral he had his cardinal's motto, *cor ad cor loquitur*, heart speaks to heart. And on the memorial tablet, by his request, were the perfectly fitting words, *ex umbris et imaginibus in veritatem*; that is, coming out of the shadows and the reflections into the truth.

Further reading

Newman's works

He collected most of them in a uniform edition of 1868 to 1881.

For the article *On Consulting the Faithful in Matters of Doctrine,* see the edition of John Coulson, 1961.

J. D. Holmes and R. D. Murray edited *On the Inspiration of Scripture*, 1967.

J. M. Cameron edited the *Essay on the development of Christian Doctrine*, 1970.

The book of private prayers was published as *Meditations and Devotions of Cardinal Newman*, 1893.

The *Apologia pro vita sua* is published in an Everyman edition; and in a modern critical edition by M. J. Svaglic, 1967 (to which my references are made). See also *My Campaign in Ireland*, 1896; and *Autobiographical Writings*, 1956.

The Idea of a University has a modern critical edition, by I. T. Ker, 1976.

A later collection of sermons (it is extraordinary how few he allowed to survive) is in *Catholic Sermons of Cardinal Newman*, 1957.

Newman's letters

C. S. Dessain and others edited excellently *The Letters and Diaries of John Henry Newman*, 31 vols, 1961– . Despite their bulk, these should on no account be neglected. Newman found it hard to write a dull letter.

Biography

Meriol Trevor's *Newman*, 2 vols, 1962, is a full, friendly and very readable biography well based on the newly available sources. C. S. Dessain's *John Henry Newman*, 3rd edition, 1980, is an unadorned short survey by the most recent master of the subject.

For the religious leadership in the Church of England, see R. W. Church, *The Oxford Movement*, 1891, a classic. It has a modern edition by G. F. A. Best, 1970.

Newman's thought

On faith: A. J. Boekraad, *The Argument from Conscience to the Existence of God, according to J. H. Newman*, 1961.

On development: Owen Chadwick, *From Bossuet to Newman*, 1957, set Newman's idea of development in its previous context, both Catholic and Protestant. Nicholas Lash, *Newman on Development*, 1975, is a direct study of Newman's idea by a philosophical theologian.

On education: A. D. Culler, *The Imperial Intellect*, 1955, is the standard study of Newman's idea of knowledge. F. McGrath's *Newman's University: Ideal and Reality*, 1951, studied the practical creation of the university in Dublin, but the book also has importance for Newman's thought.

On liberalism: T. Kenney, *The Political Thought of J. H. Newman*, 1957, is a book which will surprise those who assume that Newman never thought about politics.

The best book on Newman's idea of devotion and the life of prayer is H. C. Graef, *God and Myself: The Spirituality of J. H. Newman*, 1967.

General studies of Newman's mind are many and various. I select two older studies of especial value for different reasons. R. W. Church was Newman's close disciple during his Anglican days; and though or because he remained an Anglican, he was able to write about Newman, in *Occasional Papers*, 2 vols, 1897, with a unique combination of insight and detachment. The French ex-Jesuit Henri Bremond made himself the master of the history of Catholic spirituality. He published *The Mystery of Newman* (English translation, 1907). It has remained a controversial view, not to be accepted in all its parts. But it is the only study of Newman's mind to be itself almost a classic.

Index

Compiled by Patricia Utechin

Past Masters

AQUINAS Anthony Kenny

Anthony Kenny writes about Thomas Aquinas as a philosopher, for readers who may not share Aquinas's theological interests and beliefs. He begins with an account of Aquinas's life and works, and assesses his importance for contemporary philosophy. The book is completed by more detailed examinations of Aquinas's metaphysical system and his philosophy of mind.

'It is hard to see how such a book could be done better.' *London Review of Books*

BERKELEY J. O. Urmson

Unlike Dr Johnson in his famous jibe, J. O. Urmson achieves an unusually sympathetic assessment of Berkeley's philosophy by viewing it against a wider intellectual background than is customary. He sees Berkeley's work as a serious critical anaylsis of the scientific thought of Newton and his predecessors, and of its metaphysical basis; and he gives a clear account of the relationship between Berkeley's metaphysics and his analysis of the concepts of science and common sense.

'Professor Urmson's *Berkeley* is welcome, not just because he makes Berkeley's view that there is no such thing as matter perfectly intelligible and rather persuasive ... but because he devotes some time to explaining the moral and political positions which Berkeley thought materialism threatened.' *Listener*

CARLYLE A. L. Le Quesne

A. L. Le Quesne examines the views of this first and most influential of the Victorian 'prophets', explaining how his greatness lay in his ability to voice the needs of a remarkably moral generation.

'A first-rate introduction ... it is not the least of the merits of this excellent short study that it shows some of the tensions yet to be found in reading Carlyle.' *Edinburgh University Journal*

Past Masters

COLERIDGE Richard Holmes

Coleridge was not only a great poet, he was also a philosopher and explorer of the whole human condition. Richard Holmes describes Coleridge's work as a writer, explains his often difficult and fragmentary ideas, and shows that his concept of the creative imagination still shapes our notions of growth and culture.

'most attractive' *Listener*

'stylish, intelligent and readable' *Irish Times*

DARWIN Jonathan Howard

Darwin's theory that men's ancestors were apes caused a furore in the scientific world and outside it when *The Origin of Species* was published in 1859. Arguments still rage about the implications of his evolutionary theory, and scepticism about the value of Darwin's contribution to knowledge is widespread. In this analysis of Darwin's major insights and arguments, Jonathan Howard reasserts the importance of Darwin's work for the development of modern biology.

'Jonathan Howard has produced an intellectual *tour de force*, a classic in the genre of popular scientific exposition which will still be read in fifty years' time.' *Times Literary Supplement*

ENGELS Terrell Carver

In a sense, Engels invented Marxism. His chief intellectual legacy, the materialist interpretation of history, has had a revolutionary effect on the arts and social sciences, and his work as a whole did more than Marx's to make converts to the most influential political movement of modern times. In this book Terrell Carver traces Engels's career, and looks at the effect of the materialist interpretation of history on Marxist theory and practice.

'Carver's refreshingly honest book ... is packed with careful judgements about the different contributions of Engels to 19th century marxism.' *New Society*

Past Masters

MACHIAVELLI Quentin Skinner

Niccolò Machiavelli taught that political leaders must be prepared to do evil that good may come of it, and his name has been a byword ever since for duplicity and immorality. Is his sinister reputation really deserved? In answering this question Quentin Skinner focuses on three major works, *The Prince*, the *Discourses* and *The History of Florence*, and distils from them an introduction to Machiavelli's doctrines of exemplary clarity.

'without doubt the best short account of the author of "The Prince" that we are likely to see for some time ... a model of clarity and good judgement' *Sunday Times*

'compulsive reading' *New Society*

MARX Peter Singer

Peter Singer identifies the central vision that unifies Marx's thought, enabling us to grasp Marx's views as a whole. He views him as a philosopher primarily concerned with human freedom, rather than as an economist or social scientist. He explains alienation, historical materialism, the economic theory of *Capital*, and Marx's idea of communism, in plain English, and concludes with a balanced assessment of Marx's achievement.

'an admirably balanced portrait of the man and his achievement' *Observer*

PASCAL Alban Krailsheimer

Alban Krailsheimer opens his study of Pascal's life and work with a description of Pascal's religious conversion, and then discusses his literary, mathematical and scientific achievements, which culminated in the acute analysis of human character and powerful reasoning of the *Pensées*. He argues that after his conversion Pascal put his previous work in a different perspective and saw his, and in general all human activity, in religious terms.

'Mr Krailsheimer's enthusiasm is eloquent and infectious.' *Observer*

HO

The _____ _____ _yssey_ stand at the very beginning of Greek litera-
tur_ _ _ch has been written about their origins and authorship, but
Jasper Griffin, although he touches briefly on those questions, is here
concerned with the ideas of the poems, which have had such an incalcul-
able influence on the thought and literature of the West. He shows that
each of the two epics has its own coherent and suggestive view of the
world and of man's place within it.

'a brilliant little introduction' *The Times*

'Mr Griffin brings English scholarship up to date by bringing it firmly
back to Homer.' *London Review of Books*

JESUS Humphrey Carpenter

Humphrey Carpenter writes about Jesus from the standpoint of a
historian coming fresh to the subject without religious preconceptions.
He examines the reliability of the Gospels, the originality of Jesus's
teaching, and Jesus's view of himself. His highly readable book
achieves a remarkable degree of objectivity about a subject which is
deeply embedded in Western culture.

'Mr Carpenter has obviously made a thorough study of the latest New
Testament scholarship: but he has also read the gospels with great care,
pretending to himself that he was doing so without preconceptions, as a
historian newly presented with the source-material . . . the most extraordinary achievement.' *Observer*

A complete list of Oxford Paperbacks, including books
in the World's Classics, Past Masters and OPUS series,
can be obtained from the General Publicity Department,
Oxford University Press, Walton Street, Oxford OX2 6DP.